Unit Assessments

Mc
Graw
Hill
Education

www.mheonline.com/readingwonders

Send all inquiries to:
McGraw-Hill Education
Two Penn Plaza
New York, New York 10121

ISBN: 978-0-07-677801-0
MHID: 0-07-677801-0

Printed in the United States of America.

1 2 3 4 5 6 7 8 9 RHR 20 19 18 17 16 15
A

Table of Contents

Unit Assessments

The *Unit Assessments* component is an integral part of the complete assessment program aligned with *Reading Wonders* and state standards.

Purpose

This component reports on the outcome of student learning. As students complete each unit of the reading program, they will be assessed on their understanding of key instructional content and their ability to write to source texts/stimuli. The results serve as a summative assessment by providing a status of current achievement in relation to student progress through the curriculum. The results of the assessments can be used to inform subsequent instruction, aid in making leveling and grouping decisions, and point toward areas in need of reteaching or remediation.

Focus

Unit Assessments focuses on key areas of English Language Arts—comprehension of literature and informational text, vocabulary acquisition and use, command of the conventions of the English language, and genre writing in response to sources.

Each unit assessment also provides students familiarity with the item types, the test approaches, and the increased rigor associated with the advances in high-stakes assessment, such as the *Smarter Balanced Assessment Consortium* (SBAC) summative assessment system.

Test Administration

Each unit assessment should be administered once the instruction for the specific unit is completed. Make copies of the unit assessment for the class. You will need copies of the Answer Key pages that feature the scoring tables for each student taking the assessment. These tables provide a place to list student scores. The data from each unit assessment charts student progress and underscores strengths and weaknesses.

This component is the pencil-and-paper version of the assessment. You can administer the online version of the test, which allows for tech-enabled and tech-enhanced item functionality.

NOTE: Due to time constraints, you may wish to administer the unit assessment over multiple days. For example, students can complete Questions 1–31 on the first day and complete the Performance Task on another. For planning purposes, the recommended time for each task is 90–100 minutes over two back-to-back sessions. During the first session, provide students 30–40 minutes to read the stimulus materials and answer the research questions. During the second session, provide students 60–70 minutes for planning, writing, and editing their responses. If desired, provide students a short break between sessions. If you decide to break-up administration by assessment sections, please remember to withhold those sections of the test students are not completing to ensure test validity.

#21 in each assessment is focused on students comparing texts/writing across texts. This is a continuation of the optional activity featured in *Weekly Assessments,* and it provides valuable practice for the type of critical thinking and writing required in performance-based assessments. If you feel students have adequate exposure to this writing performance in the tasks and removing the item will reduce test administration time, you can decide not to administer item #21 and remove that page from the test packet. Deleting the item will result in a 50-point skill test; note this deletion in your scoring tables.

Teacher Introduction

After each student has a copy of the assessment, provide a version of the following directions:

Say: *Write your name and the date on the question pages for this assessment.* (When students are finished, continue with the directions.) *You will read four texts and answer questions about them. In the next part of the test, you will read drafts and/or passages. You will revise these or edit for the correct grammar, mechanics, and usage. In the final part of the test, you will read sources, answer questions about them, and write a response based on the assignment you will find, an assignment that will ask you to use those sources in your writing.*

Read each part of the test carefully. For multiple-choice items, completely fill in the circle next to the correct answer or answers. For items that ask you to write on the page, look carefully at the directions to answer the question. You may be asked to match items, circle or underline choices, complete a chart, or place details in order. For constructed response items, write your response on the lines provided. For the performance tasks, write your response to the assignment on clean sheets of paper. When you have completed the assessment, put your pencil down and turn the pages over. You may begin now.

Answer procedural questions during the assessment, but do not provide any assistance on the items or selections. Have extra paper on hand for students to use for their task responses. After the class has completed the assessment, ask students to verify that their names and the date are written on the necessary pages.

Assessment Items

Unit assessments feature the following item types—selected response (SR), multiple selected response (MSR), evidence-based selected response (EBSR), constructed response (CR), technology-enhanced items (TE), and extended constructed response (ECR). (Please note that the print versions of TE items are available in this component; the full functionality of the items is available only through the online assessment.) This variety of item types provides multiple methods of assessing student understanding, allows for deeper investigation into skills and strategies, and provides students an opportunity to become familiar with the kinds of questions they will encounter in state-mandated summative assessments.

Performance Tasks

Each unit features a Performance Task (PT) assessment in a previously-taught genre. Students will complete two examples of each type by the end of the year.

The task types are:

- Informational
  - Students generate a thesis based on the sources and use information from the sources to explain this thesis.
- Narrative
  - Students craft a narrative using information from the sources.
- Opinion
  - Students analyze the ideas in sources and make a claim that they support using the sources.

Each PT assesses standards that address comprehension, research skills, genre writing, and the use of standard English language conventions (ELC). The stimulus texts and research questions in each task build toward the goal of the final writing topic.

Copyright © McGraw-Hill Education

Teacher Introduction

Overview

- Students will read four texts in each assessment and respond to items focusing on Comprehension Skills, Literary Elements, Text Features, and Vocabulary Strategies. These items assess the ability to access meaning from the text and demonstrate understanding of unknown and multiple-meaning words and phrases.
- Students will then read a draft that requires corrections or clarifications to its use of the conventions of standard English language and/or complete a cloze passage that requires correct usage identification.
- Students are then presented with a Performance Task assignment.

Each test item in *Unit Assessments* (as well as in weekly and benchmark assessments) has a Depth of Knowledge (DOK) level assigned to it.

DOK 1 in vocabulary involves students using word parts (affixes, roots, and so on) to determine the meaning of an unknown word or non-contextual items assessing synonym/ antonym and multiple-meaning words.

DOK 2 in vocabulary involves students using context to determine the meaning of an unknown word and dealing with figurative language in context.

DOK 1 in comprehension involves students identifying/locating information in the text.

DOK 2 in comprehension involves students analyzing text structures/story elements.

DOK 3 in comprehension involves students making inferences using text evidence and analyzing author's craft.

DOK 4 in comprehension involves using multiple stimulus texts and writing across texts.

DOK 1 in ELC/PTs involves students editing to fix errors.

DOK 2 in ELC/PTs involves students revising and planning writing or investigating sources.

DOK 3 and *DOK 4* in ELC/PTs involve research and student full-writes.

Each unit assessment features four "Cold Reads" on which the comprehension and vocabulary assessment items are based. These selections reflect the unit theme to support the focus of the classroom instruction. Texts fall within the Lexile band 830L-1010L. Complexity on this quantitative measure grows throughout the units, unless a qualitative measure supports text placement outside a lockstep Lexile continuum.

Comprehension

Comprehension items in each unit assess student understanding of the text through the use of the Comprehension Skills, Literary Elements, and Text Features.

Vocabulary

Vocabulary items ask students to demonstrate the ability to uncover the meanings of unknown and multiple-meaning words and phrases using Vocabulary Strategies.

English Language Conventions

A total of ten items in each unit ask students to demonstrate their command of the conventions of standard English.

Performance Task

Students complete one task per unit, the final result being a written product in the specified task genre.

Teacher Introduction

Scoring

Use the scoring tables to assign final unit assessment scores. Each part of an EBSR is worth 1 point; MSR and TECR items should be answered correctly in full, though you may choose to provide partial credit.

For written responses, use the correct response parameters provided in the Answer Key and the scoring rubrics listed below to assign a score. Responses that show a complete lack of understanding or are left blank should be given a *0*.

Short Response Score: 2

The response is well-crafted and concise and shows a thorough understanding of the underlying skill. Appropriate text evidence is used to answer the question.

Short Response Score: 1

The response shows partial understanding of the underlying skill. Text evidence is featured, though examples are too general.

Extended Response Score: 4

- The student understands the question/prompt and responds suitably using the appropriate text evidence from the selection or selections.
- The response is an acceptably complete answer to the question/prompt.
- The organization of the response is meaningful.
- The response stays on-topic; ideas are linked to one another with effective transitions.
- The response has correct spelling, grammar, usage, and mechanics.

Extended Response Score: 3

- The student understands the question/prompt and responds suitably using the appropriate text evidence from the selection or selections.
- The response is a somewhat complete answer to the question/prompt.
- The organization of the response is somewhat meaningful.
- The response maintains focus; ideas are linked to one another.
- The response has occasional errors in spelling, grammar, usage, and mechanics.

Extended Response Score: 2

- The student has partial understanding of the question/prompt and uses some text evidence.
- The response is an incomplete answer to the question/prompt.
- The organization of the response is weak.
- The writing is careless; contains extraneous information and ineffective transitions.
- The response requires effort to read easily.
- The response has noticeable errors in spelling, grammar, usage, and mechanics.

Extended Response Score: 1

- The student has minimal understanding of the question/prompt and uses little to no appropriate text evidence.
- The response is a barely acceptable answer to the question/prompt.
- The response lacks organization.
- The writing is erratic with little focus; ideas are not connected to each other.
- The response is difficult to follow.
- The response has frequent errors in spelling, grammar, usage, and mechanics.

Teacher Introduction

Use the rubrics to score the task holistically on a 10-point scale: 4 points for purpose/organization [P/O]; 4 points for evidence/elaboration [E/E] or development/elaboration [D/E]; and 2 points for English language conventions [C]

Unscorable or **Zero** responses are unrelated to the topic, illegible, contain little or no writing, or show little to no command of the conventions of standard English.

INFORMATIVE PERFORMANCE TASK SCORING RUBRIC

Score	Purpose/Organization	Evidence/Elaboration	Conventions
4	• **effective** organizational structure • clear statement of main idea based on purpose, audience, task • consistent use of various transitions • logical progression of ideas	• **convincing** support for main idea; **effective** use of sources • integrates comprehensive evidence from sources • relevant references • effective use of elaboration • audience-appropriate domain-specific vocabulary	
3	• **evident** organizational structure • adequate statement of main idea based on purpose, audience, task • adequate, somewhat varied use of transitions • adequate progression of ideas	• **adequate** support for main idea; **adequate** use of sources • some integration of evidence from sources • references may be general • adequate use of some elaboration • generally audience-appropriate domain-specific vocabulary	
2	• **inconsistent** organizational structure • unclear or somewhat unfocused main idea • inconsistent use of transitions with little variety • formulaic or uneven progression of ideas	• **uneven** support for main idea; **limited** use of sources • weakly integrated, vague, or imprecise evidence from sources • references are vague or absent • weak or uneven elaboration • uneven domain-specific vocabulary	• **adequate** command of spelling, capitalization, punctuation, grammar, and usage • few errors
1	• **little or no** organizational structure • few or no transitions • frequent extraneous ideas; may be formulaic • may lack introduction and/or conclusion • confusing or ambiguous focus; may be very brief	• **minimal** support for main idea; **little or no** use of sources • minimal, absent, incorrect, or irrelevant evidence from sources • references are absent or incorrect • minimal, if any, elaboration • limited or ineffective domain-specific vocabulary	• **partial** command of spelling, capitalization, punctuation, grammar, and usage • some patterns of errors

Teacher Introduction

NARRATIVE PERFORMANCE TASK SCORING RUBRIC

Score	Purpose/Organization	Development/Elaboration	Conventions
4	• **fully sustained** organization; **clear** focus • effective, unified plot • effective development of setting, characters, point of view • transitions clarify relationships between and among ideas • logical sequence of events • effective opening and closing	• **effective** elaboration with details, dialogue, description • clear expression of experiences and events • effective use of relevant source material • effective use of various narrative techniques • effective use of sensory, concrete, and figurative language	
3	• **adequately sustained** organization; **generally maintained** focus • evident plot with loose connections • adequate development of setting, characters, point of view • adequate use of transitional strategies • adequate sequence of events • adequate opening and closing	• **adequate** elaboration with details, dialogue, description • adequate expression of experiences and events • adequate use of source material • adequate use of various narrative techniques • adequate use of sensory, concrete, and figurative language	
2	• **somewhat sustained** organization; **uneven** focus • inconsistent plot with evident flaws • uneven development of setting, characters, point of view • uneven use of transitional strategies, with little variety • weak or uneven sequence of events • weak opening and closing	• **uneven** elaboration with **partial** details, dialogue, description • uneven expression of experiences and events • vague, abrupt, or imprecise use of source material • uneven, inconsistent use of narrative technique • partial or weak use of sensory, concrete, and figurative language	• **adequate** command of spelling, capitalization, punctuation, grammar, and usage • few errors
1	• **basic** organization; **little or no** focus • little or no discernible plot; may just be a series of events • brief or no development of setting, characters, point of view • few or no transitional strategies • little or no organization of event sequence; extraneous ideas • no opening and/or closing	• **minimal** elaboration with **few or no** details, dialogue, description • confusing expression of experiences and events • little or no use of source material • minimal or incorrect use of narrative techniques • little or no use of sensory, concrete, and figurative language	• **partial** command of spelling, capitalization, punctuation, grammar, and usage • some patterns of errors

Teacher Introduction

OPINION PERFORMANCE TASK SCORING RUBRIC

Score	Purpose/Organization	Evidence/Elaboration	Conventions
4	• **effective** organizational structure; **sustained** focus • consistent use of various transitions • logical progression of ideas • effective introduction and conclusion • clearly communicated opinion for purpose, audience, task	• **convincing** support/evidence for main idea; **effective** use of sources; **precise** language • comprehensive evidence from sources is integrated • relevant, specific references • effective elaborative techniques • appropriate domain-specific vocabulary for audience, purpose	
3	• **evident** organizational structure; **adequate** focus • adequate use of transitions • adequate progression of ideas • adequate introduction and conclusion • clear opinion, mostly maintained, though loosely • adequate opinion for purpose, audience, task	• **adequate** support/evidence for main idea; **adequate** use of sources; **general** language • some evidence from sources is integrated • general, imprecise references • adequate elaboration • generally appropriate domain-specific vocabulary for audience, purpose	
2	• **inconsistent** organizational structure; **somewhat sustained** focus • inconsistent use of transitions • uneven progression of ideas • introduction or conclusion, if present, may be weak • somewhat unclear or unfocused opinion	• **uneven** support for main idea; **partial** use of sources; **simple** language • evidence from sources is weakly integrated, vague, or imprecise • vague, unclear references • weak or uneven elaboration • uneven or somewhat ineffective use of domain-specific vocabulary for audience, purpose	• **adequate** command of spelling, capitalization, punctuation, grammar, and usage • few errors
1	• **little or no** organizational structure or focus • few or no transitions • frequent extraneous ideas are evident; may be formulaic • introduction and/or conclusion may be missing • confusing opinion	• **minimal** support for main idea; **little or no** use of sources; **vague** language • source material evidence is minimal, incorrect, or irrelevant • references absent or incorrect • minimal, if any, elaboration • limited or ineffective use of domain-specific vocabulary for audience, purpose	• **partial** command of spelling, capitalization, punctuation, grammar, and usage • some patterns of errors

Teacher Introduction

Evaluating Scores

The goal of each unit assessment is to evaluate student mastery of previously-taught material. The expectation is for students to score 80% or higher on the assessment as a whole. Within this score, the expectation is for students to score 75% or higher on each section of the assessment.

For students who do not meet these benchmarks, assign appropriate lessons from the Tier 2 online PDFs. Refer to the unit assessment pages in the Teacher's Edition of *Reading Wonders* for specific lessons.

The Answer Keys have been constructed to provide the information you need to aid your understanding of student performance, as well as individualized instructional and intervention needs.

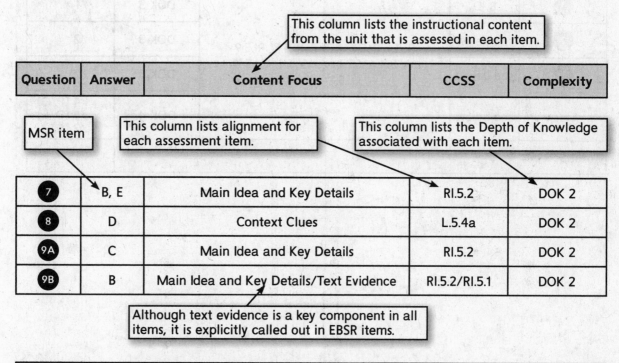

This column lists the instructional content from the unit that is assessed in each item.

Question	Answer	Content Focus	CCSS	Complexity

MSR item

This column lists alignment for each assessment item.

This column lists the Depth of Knowledge associated with each item.

Question	Answer	Content Focus	CCSS	Complexity
7	B, E	Main Idea and Key Details	RI.5.2	DOK 2
8	D	Context Clues	L.5.4a	DOK 2
9A	C	Main Idea and Key Details	RI.5.2	DOK 2
9B	B	Main Idea and Key Details/Text Evidence	RI.5.2/RI.5.1	DOK 2

Although text evidence is a key component in all items, it is explicitly called out in EBSR items.

Comprehension: Selected Response 4A, 4B, 5A, 5B, 6A, 6B, 8A, 8B, 10A, 10B, 16A, 16B, 19A, 19B	/14	%
Comprehension: Constructed Response 7, 12, 14, 17, 20, 21	/14	%
Vocabulary 1, 2A, 2B, 3, 9A, 9B, 11, 13, 15, 18	/16	%
English Language Conventions 22-31	/10	%
Total Unit Assessment Score	/54	%

Scoring rows identify items by assessment focus and item type and allow for quick record keeping.

Teacher Introduction

Evaluating Scores

For PTs, SR items are worth 1 point each. CR items are worth 2 points each.

Use the rubrics to score the full-write.

An anchor paper response can be found in each unit. This top-line response is included to assist with scoring.

The expectation is for students to score 12/15 on the entire task, and 8/10 on the full-write.

Narrative Performance Task					
Question	**Answer**	**CCSS**		**Complexity**	**Score**
1	B, D	RI.5.1, RI.5.2; RI.5.7, RI.5.8, RI.5.9 W.5.2, W.5.3a-e, W.5.4, W.5.7 L.5.1, L.5.2		DOK 3	/1
2	see below			DOK 3	/2
3	see below			DOK 3	/2
Story	see below			DOK 4	/4 [P/O] /4 [D/E] /2 [C]
Total Score					/15

Read the text. Then answer the questions.

Camping Without a Phone

I couldn't believe it when my parents told me we were spending our winter vacation going camping! They are always trying to get me to go outside more. It seems like my mom is constantly saying, "Brian, turn off the computer!" or "Brian, put down your phone and talk to us!" They don't seem to understand that I'm in the zone when I'm using a keyboard, so of course I don't want to stop.

We drove for an hour to Everglades National Park. As soon as we got there, my cell phone stopped working. The precaution I had taken of fully charging it had done no good. I couldn't get a signal for it. Suddenly, I was facing three days of no contact with the outside world. My little brother, Ben, thought it was amusing, and my mom tried to convince me I'd like it. "You'll be able to look around more when you're not staring at a screen," she said.

"You might have to act like a human being," said Ben as he started laughing. Then he escaped to the other side of the campground.

We took a hike with a ranger in the afternoon. At first, I couldn't care less, but after a while I started paying attention. By the end of the hike, I realized there was more action going on in the park than in most video games. It just didn't happen as obviously.

First, the ranger explained that fires can be beneficial for the Everglades. Lightning starts the fires. The pines and some other trees resist fire, and their branches are too high for the fires to reach. Other trees and plants that try to take over from the pines are lower and get burned away. I could almost envision the fires burning around us while we walked, as if they were on a video screen.

GO ON →

Then we stopped to look at a pile of fur and little bones, apparently left behind by a bobcat. They were probably the remains of a rabbit. The ranger said that bobcats hunt nearly every night and sometimes eat animals as large as a deer. Unfortunately we didn't get to see the action, but we saw some of the results.

Then we saw a wood stork wading and moving its beak back and forth. It was over three feet tall. Because the water is muddy and full of plants, it can't see the small fish it's trying to catch. But its beak is very sensitive. When it touches a fish, its beak snaps closed in 25 milliseconds! That's faster than some computer networks respond when I touch a key.

That night I was exhausted from walking all day, and because I didn't use enough sunscreen I looked a little like what the ranger called the "tourist tree." The gumbo limbo tree has reddish bark that peels off, like it got sunburned. Even so, I woke up in the middle of the night, and I was terrified at first because of some mysterious sounds. But then I recognized the barred owl the ranger had described to us earlier that day. It sounds like it's calling out "Who cooks for you? Who cooks for you?" That helped me to relax, so I was able to fall back to sleep.

We spent a lot of time exploring over the next two days. I started to understand the connection between the land and water and animals. In the Everglades, you couldn't even get rid of the mosquitoes without creating a big change for other animals. Small fish eat mosquito eggs; other fish eat the smaller fish; large fish called gars eat those fish; and alligators eat the gars. If you eliminated the mosquitoes, you might lose some of the other animals higher up the food chain too.

After we left, we talked in the car about the Everglades and how different it was from where we lived. Suddenly, right in the middle of our discussion, I heard a familiar tone from my phone. My friend Jeff was sending me a text. Without thinking, I reached for my phone, but then I put it back down. "Aren't you going to text back?" asked Ben.

"I will in a little while," I said. Ben looked stunned. My dad and mom looked at each other and just smiled.

GO ON →

1 Read the sentence from the text.

They don't seem to understand that I'm <u>in the zone</u> when I'm using a keyboard, so of course I don't want to stop.

What does the phrase "in the zone" suggest about Brian? Select **two** options.

(A) He is happy.

(B) He is a hard worker.

(C) He is an excellent typist.

(D) He is angry at his parents.

(E) He is trying to get started.

(F) He is focused on what he is doing.

2 Read the sentence from the text.

The <u>precaution</u> I had taken of fully charging it had done no good.

The prefix *pre-* means before. What does the word <u>precaution</u> mean?

(A) warned others

(B) planned ahead

(C) was not warned

(D) planned many times

GO ON →

3 The following question has two parts. First, answer part A. Then, answer part B.

Part A: Read the sentence from the text.

I could almost <u>envision</u> the fires burning around us while we walked, as if they were on a video screen.

What does <u>envision</u> mean in the sentence above?

(A) hear

(B) feel

(C) see

(D) smell

Part B: What phrase from the sentence **best** supports your answer in part A?

(A) "could almost"

(B) "fires burning around us"

(C) "while we walked"

(D) "video screen"

GO ON →

4 The following question has two parts. First, answer part A. Then, answer part B.

Part A: Where do most of the events in the text take place?

(A) a national park

(B) the family car

(C) a ranger station

(D) Brian's house

Part B: Which detail from the text **best** supports your answer in part A?

(A) "They are always trying to get me to go outside more."

(B) "Then we saw a wood stork wading and moving its beak back and forth."

(C) "After we left, we talked in the car about the Everglades and how different it was from where we lived."

(D) Suddenly, right in the middle of our discussion, I heard a familiar tone from my phone.

GO ON →

5 The following question has two parts. First, answer part A. Then, answer part B.

Part A: How does Brian's inability to use his cell phone while camping affect his actions?

(A) It helps him prove to his family that he can survive in the Everglades.

(B) It allows him to better understand technology.

(C) It forces him to participate in new activities.

(D) It gives him the chance to improve his relationship with his brother.

Part B: Which detail from the passage **best** supports your answer in part A?

(A) "'You might have to act like a human being,' said Ben as he started laughing."

(B) "By the end of the hike, I realized there was more action going on in the park than in most video games."

(C) "That helped me to relax, so I was able to fall back to sleep."

(D) "That's faster than some computer networks respond when I touch a key."

GO ON →

6 The following question has two parts. First, answer part A. Then, answer part B.

Part A: Which statement **best** explains how Brian's problem is solved?

(A) He discovers things that interest him.

(B) He finds out how his family **feels** about him.

(C) He sees that his cell service has returned.

(D) He learns how to respond to danger at the park.

Part B: Which sentence from the text supports your answer in part A?

(A) "We drove for an hour to Everglades National Park."

(B) "Suddenly, I was facing three days of no contact with the outside world."

(C) At first, I couldn't care less, but after a while I started paying attention.

(D) "My friend Jeff was sending me a text."

GO ON →

7 Read the paragraphs from the text.

After we left, we talked in the car about the Everglades and how different it was from where we lived. Suddenly, right in the middle of our discussion, I heard a familiar tone from my phone. My friend Jeff was sending me a text. Without thinking, I reached for my phone, but then I put it back down. 'Aren't you going to text back?' asked Ben.

"I will in a little while," I said. Ben looked stunned. My dad and mom looked at each other and just smiled.

Why do Brian's parents smile at each other? Support your answer with details from the text.

_____

_____

_____

_____

_____

Read the text. Then answer the questions.

Breaking Barriers

Elizabeth Blackwell listened to her friend's unusual advice. He said that she should disguise herself as a man if she wanted to study and become a doctor! It was 1845, and only men attended medical school. However, Elizabeth absolutely refused to participate in the dishonest scheme. She wanted the world to know that a woman could be a capable doctor, too.

Childhood Lessons

Elizabeth was born in England in 1821. At that time, few women focused on school studies. Fortunately, Elizabeth's father believed that women should have a wide education. He hired tutors to teach all his children challenging subjects like mathematics and Latin. Elizabeth loved learning, and she developed a passion for reading.

When Elizabeth was 11 years old, her family moved to America. She continued her education, attending an excellent school. When she was just 16, she became a teacher. It was one of the few acceptable careers for a woman. Elizabeth was skilled at her job, but she felt restless. One day, a sick woman inspired Elizabeth to pursue a new goal. She suggested that Elizabeth use her sharp mind to become a doctor.

Battling for a Chance

Elizabeth's close friends gently told her that her new dream was impossible for a woman, but Elizabeth was not discouraged. She began reading and studying medical textbooks. One doctor, persuaded by her dedication, let Elizabeth attend his medical lectures and use his library. At the same time, Elizabeth sent in applications to medical schools around the country.

Sadly, Elizabeth received 16 letters of rejection. Finally, the Geneva Medical College in New York accepted her as a student. Elizabeth did not know it, but the male students at the school thought her letter was a silly joke. When asked by teachers to vote on the issue, they laughed and shouted, "Yes."

GO ON →

Classroom Struggles

At the college, Elizabeth concentrated on her studies. If paper airplanes winged her way, she brushed them aside. When professors told her a woman should not witness certain operations, she wrote letters to convince them otherwise. When people in town ignored the woman with the strange ambition, Elizabeth treated them in a polite, quiet manner.

As the weeks passed, Elizabeth's fellow students grew to respect and admire their hardworking classmate. Two years later, Elizabeth graduated at the top of her class. She became the first woman in the country to obtain a medical degree.

Changing Views

The newspapers wrote favorably about Elizabeth's achievement, and the public was impressed. Like a small crack in a dike, Elizabeth's success opened the way for others. In the next few years, several more medical schools accepted women students. The views of a woman's abilities were shifting.

Throughout her life, Elizabeth continued to be a pioneer in the medical field. She championed the education of women and their care. She also directed attention at preventing disease by teaching others about washing hands. Always, Elizabeth faced any challenges with determination. She once wrote that if an idea was valuable, "there must be some way of realizing it!"

GO ON →

8 Read the sentence from the text.

However, Elizabeth absolutely refused to participate in the dishonest scheme.

Which word from the sentence helps explain what dishonest means?

(A) absolutely

(B) refused

(C) participate

(D) scheme

9 How does the author support the idea that Elizabeth's father influenced her future career as a doctor? Support your answer with details from the text.

_____

_____

_____

_____

_____

_____

GO ON →

10 Read the sentence from the text.

One day, a sick woman inspired Elizabeth to <u>pursue</u> a new goal.

What does the word pursue **most likely** mean in the sentence above?

(A) follow close behind

(B) create a change

(C) learn all about

(D) try to achieve

11 Read the sentence from the text.

One doctor, <u>persuaded by her dedication</u>, let Elizabeth attend his medical lectures and use his library.

What does the use of the phrase "persuaded by her dedication" suggest? Select **two** options.

(A) Elizabeth did not give up.

(B) Elizabeth liked to complain.

(C) The doctor felt sorry for her.

(D) Elizabeth did not have a lot of money.

(E) The doctor was impressed by her work.

(F) Elizabeth was smarter than the other students.

GO ON →

12 The following question has two parts. First, answer part A. Then, answer part B.

Part A: How did Elizabeth respond to the obstacles she faced at the medical college?

(A) She kept trying even when people opposed her.

(B) She became friendly with her classmates.

(C) She studied longer than her classmates in order to graduate.

(D) She tried to prove she was the smartest student in the class.

Part B: Which sentence from the text **best** supports your answer in part A?

(A) "At the college, Elizabeth concentrated on her studies."

(B) "When professors told her a woman should not witness certain operations, she wrote letters to convince them otherwise."

(C) "As the weeks passed, Elizabeth's fellow students grew to respect and admire their hardworking classmate."

(D) "Two years later, Elizabeth graduated at the top of her class."

GO ON →

13 The following question has two parts. First, answer part A. Then, answer part B.

Part A: Why did the author **most likely** choose the title "Breaking Barriers" for this text?

(A) to show that Elizabeth worked hard to make people like her

(B) to show that Elizabeth accomplished things never done before

(C) to show that Elizabeth proved to be smarter than those around her

(D) to show that Elizabeth tried to show she was the better than other doctors

Part B: Which sentences from the text **best** support your answer in part A? Select **two** options.

(A) "Elizabeth loved learning, and she developed a passion for reading."

(B) "When Elizabeth was 11 years old, her family moved to America."

(C) "When she was just 16, she became a teacher."

(D) "Finally, the Geneva Medical College in New York accepted her as a student."

(E) "When people in town ignored the woman with the strange ambition, Elizabeth treated them in a polite, quiet manner."

(F) "She became the first woman in the country to obtain a medical degree."

GO ON →

14 The following question has two parts. First, answer part A. Then, answer part B.

Part A: Why does the author describe the attitudes of the public and Elizabeth's professors?

(A) to show the struggles Elizabeth's faced in her life

(B) to describe how Elizabeth's achievements made her famous

(C) to explain how Elizabeth proved to people that women were fine teachers

(D) to demonstrate that Elizabeth helped people accept the idea of women doctors

Part B: Which sentence from the text **best** supports your answer in part A?

(A) "The newspapers wrote favorably about Elizabeth's achievement, and the public was impressed."

(B) "In the next few years, several more medical schools accepted women students."

(C) "She also directed attention at preventing disease by teaching others about washing hands."

(D) "Always, Elizabeth faced any challenges with determination."

GO ON →

Read the texts. Then answer the questions.

Sailing the Seas

Put together wood and canvas. Power them with wind. What do you get? You have created the sailing ship. For thousands of years, the sailing ship was the main way to travel the ocean. Early explorers used their knowledge of astronomy to guide them as they traveled on sailing ships to visit other lands and map the world. People used sailing ships to trade with other countries. People also used sailing ships to travel across oceans to settle new lands.

Beginning in the 1840s, a new type of ship began to sail the seas. It was called a clipper ship. Clipper ships were among the most beautiful sailing vessels ever built. They had long, narrow bodies and tall masts to hold their many sails. When the wind filled their sails, clipper ships seemed to fly across the water.

Clipper ships were built to be faster than other sailing ships. Before clipper ships, it could take 200 days to travel from New York to California. Clipper ships could make the trip in less than 100 days.

Shipbuilders competed to build the fastest clipper ships. Donald McKay was the best designer and builder of clipper ships. He learned to build ships when he was in the navy and then ran a shipyard in Massachusetts. Between the launching of his first ship in 1845 and the closing of his shipyard in 1873, McKay built some of the largest and fastest clipper ships. One of McKay's ships, the *Flying Cloud*, set a record for the fastest trip from New York to California. In 1854, it made the trip in 86 days.

GO ON →

Clipper ships were used to transport goods around the world. They carried tea and silk from China to New York and California. Clippers also moved goods produced on the East Coast to gold miners and settlers in California. The cargo on a clipper ship was valuable. One clipper ship, the *Challenger*, returned from China carrying silk and tea worth $2 million.

In the 1860s, new forms of transportation began to replace the clipper ship. Railroads were built across the United States so people could use trains to ship goods. Steamships were also invented. Steamships had a big advantage over clipper ships and other sailing ships. They did not have to depend on wind for the power to propel them. They had engines powered by steam. Steamships could run in a greater variety of weather conditions, so they were more reliable than clipper ships. Then, as now, traders wanted to beat their competitors. They wanted to arrive at their destinations before anyone else and with the most cargo. So, of course, they turned to steam-powered vessels. In a short time, the age of the sailing ship had ended.

GO ON →

Fulton's Triumph

A nervous crowd moved about on a dock on the East River in New York City on August 17, 1807. Robert Fulton was set to make a trip up the Hudson River to Albany and had chosen several brave friends to go with him. It would be the first trip of its kind on a boat powered by a steam engine.

When the boat was being built, Fulton often noticed people making fun of it and joking about it. The boat was big-about 150 feet long-but it didn't look like other ships of the time. It was only 13 feet wide, and it had just one small sail and a flat bottom. A large paddle wheel stuck out on both sides. People thought it was misnamed the *North River* and should have been called *Fulton's Folly* because it was so foolish.

When it was time to begin the trip, Fulton's friends looked worried. Things did not get better when the *North River* stopped moving only a short way from the dock. Some of the passengers grumbled and wished they had not come.

Fulton was able to fix the problem with a minor adjustment. Soon the boat was rapidly moving up the river. It made its first stop at the town of *Clermont*. Later, people gave the boat the name of the town, Clermont. It traveled the first 110 miles in just 24 hours. Fulton reported passing many schooners so quickly that they seemed as if they were anchored. In another eight hours, the boat arrived in Albany.

The passengers gladly left the boat for dry land. They were thankful they had made it safely. Still, they told Fulton he probably couldn't do it again. Even if he could, they thought it would be unimportant to people.

Fulton posted a sign seeking passengers for the return trip to New York. He would charge $3, the same price as the sailing ships. Only two passengers signed up. Most people were afraid the steam boiler would explode. The crew fed a roaring fire with pine logs. The tall chimney spouted a dense stream of black smoke and steady shower of sparks. One observer thought the boat looked like a sawmill mounted on a flat-bottomed boat and set on fire.

GO ON →

The steamboat looked very different from the silent, majestic sailing ships of the time, especially at night. The crews of some sailing ships thought it was a monster racing down the river. They hid below the deck when it passed. Other people stood on the banks, waving handkerchiefs and cheering in celebration.

Fulton and his passengers arrived back in New York City safely. The boat had covered 300 miles in 62 hours, a little more than 2 ½ days. Sailing ships traveled the same route in about seven days. Gradually, people became less frightened, and Fulton's business grew. People were willing to pay high prices for the quick trip on the Hudson. Land travel was slow and uncomfortable. Shifting winds and tides made sailing the river unpredictable. Within a year, Fulton's company was earning $1,000 a week, and Fulton soon became one of the richest people in the country.

Fulton and others improved the design of the steamboats and made them more comfortable for passengers. One steamboat towed barges that contained sleeping rooms. Before, people had slept above the boilers. With this new boat, passengers could sleep well away from the dangers of the fire.

Within 15 years of Fulton's first voyage, at least 69 steamboats were churning up and down the Mississippi and Ohio Rivers. About 15 years after that, new steamships were designed to undertake ocean voyages. Fulton did not invent the steamboat, but he made it an economic success. Today, his first boat might be called *Fulton's Triumph* rather than *Fulton's Folly*.

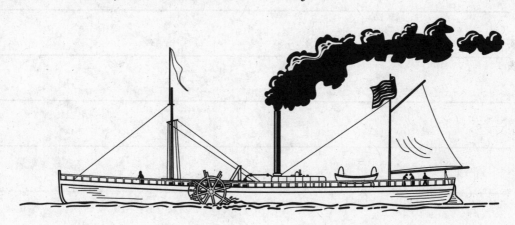

GO ON →

Answer these questions about "Sailing the Seas."

15 How does the author explain the end of the age of the sailing ship?

- (A) by comparing sailing ships to railroads
- (B) by describing a sequence of events in transportation
- (C) by listing the problems caused by clipper ships and describing the solutions
- (D) by describing what caused people to turn to new forms of transportation

16 Read the sentences from the text

Then, as now, traders wanted to beat their competitors. They wanted to arrive at their destinations before anyone else and with the most cargo. So, of course, they turned to steam-powered vessels. In a short time, the age of the sailing ship had ended.

What conclusion can be drawn about the author's point of view? Support your answer with details from the text.

_____

_____

_____

_____

_____

GO ON →

17 Read the sentence from the text.

Early explorers used their knowledge of <u>astronomy</u> to guide them as they traveled on sailing ships to visit other lands and map the world.

The word *astronomy* is based on a Greek root meaning "star." What does the word astronomy **most likely** mean?

(A) travel through space

(B) making maps

(C) study of the stars

(D) building ships

GO ON →

Answer these questions about "Fulton's Triumph."

18 The following question has two parts. First, answer part A. Then, answer part B.

Part A: Read the sentence from the text.

When the boat was being built, Fulton often noticed people <u>making fun of it</u> and joking about it.

What does the idiom "making fun of" mean?

(A) laughing at

(B) being happy about

(C) inventing names for

(D) creating a new game

Part B: Which words from the sentence **best** support your answer in Part A?

(A) "When the boat"

(B) "was being built"

(C) "often noticed people"

(D) "joking about it"

19 Draw a line between each statement and the reason that **best** explains why the author included it in the text.

"One observer thought the boat looked like a sawmill mounted on a flat-bottomed boat and set on fire."	to explain why Fulton's business grew
	to explain why the steamboat seemed dangerous
"Land travel was slow and uncomfortable. Shifting winds and tides made sailing the river unpredictable."	to explain the challenges Fulton faced
	to explain why the steamboat did not rely on solar power

GO ON →

20 Read the sentence from the text.

Today, his boat might be called *Fulton's Triumph* rather than *Fulton's Folly*.

Explain what this sentence shows about the author's point of view. Use details from the text to support your response.

_____

_____

_____

_____

_____

GO ON →

Now answer this question about "Sailing the Seas" and "Fulton's Triumph."

21 The introduction of clipper ships and steamboats brought about major changes in transportation. Explain these changes, using at least **two** details from **each** text.

_____

_____

_____

_____

_____

_____

_____

_____

_____

_____

_____

_____

_____

GO ON →

The text below needs revision. Read the text. Then answer the questions.

(1) I started playing football on a new team this year, our coach gave us a notebook with plays in it. (2) I looked at the pages, but I didn't understand anything. (3) The coach showed us the book and explained about the drawings. (4) they were all X's, O's, and arrows. (5) When I looked at them, they just looked like someone had scribbled on the paper!

(6) When we played the first game. (7) I didn't know where to line up or where to go when the play started. (8) Finally, the coach had to take me out of the game.

(9) That night I asked my dad to help me. (10) He explained and pointed with his fingers, but it still didn't make sense. (11) I got so frustrated, I yelled, "No, I can't learn this!" (12) Then I ran up to my room.

(13) I came back down my dad had checkers spread out on the table. (14) Our team was red, and the other team was black. (15) I was the player that was two checkers high. (16) He started to move the checkers around like a football play. (17) Suddenly, I got it!

(18) I told the coach before the next game and he let me play. (19) I knew what to do. (20) That day we played checkers. (21) I've had a good season.

GO ON →

22 What is the **best** way to correct sentence 1?

(A) I started playing football on a new team this year. Our coach gave us a notebook with plays in it.

(B) I started playing football on a new team this year: our coach gave us a notebook with plays in it.

(C) I started playing football. On a new team this year, our coach gave us a notebook with plays in it.

(D) I started playing football on a new team this year. our coach gave us a notebook with plays in it.

23 Which sentence has an error in capitalization?

(A) Sentence 2

(B) Sentence 3

(C) Sentence 4

(D) Sentence 5

24 Which sentence includes an interjection?

(A) Sentence 5

(B) Sentence 8

(C) Sentence 11

(D) Sentence 16

25 Which of these is a sentence fragment?

(A) Sentence 6

(B) Sentence 7

(C) Sentence 8

(D) Sentence 9

GO ON →

26 Which sentence has a compound predicate?

- Ⓐ Sentence 3
- Ⓑ Sentence 5
- Ⓒ Sentence 8
- Ⓓ Sentence 12

27 What is the **best** way to write sentence 13?

- Ⓐ I came back down, then my dad had checkers spread out on the table.
- Ⓑ I came back down, my dad had checkers spread out on the table.
- Ⓒ Because I came back down, my dad had checkers spread out on the table.
- Ⓓ When I came back down, my dad had checkers spread out on the table.

28 Which of these is a compound sentence?

- Ⓐ Sentence 5
- Ⓑ Sentence 6
- Ⓒ Sentence 9
- Ⓓ Sentence 14

29 What is the subject of sentence 17?

- Ⓐ Suddenly
- Ⓑ I
- Ⓒ got
- Ⓓ it

GO ON →

30 What is the **best** way to write sentence 18?

(A) I told the coach before the next game. And he let me play.

(B) I told the coach before the next game, and he let me play.

(C) I told the coach before the next game, he let me play.

(D) I told the coach before the next game but he let me play.

31 What is the **best** way to combine sentences 20 and 21?

(A) Playing checkers made me have a good season.

(B) Although I've had a good season, that day we played checkers.

(C) That day we played checkers because I've had a good season.

(D) Since that day we played checkers, I've had a good season.

STOP

Narrative Performance Task

Task:

Your class has been learning about how challenges can bring out the best in people. Now your school is having a writing competition. Each student in your school is going write a story to submit to the principal about their idea for a monument that will honor a local hero. Before you begin to work on your story, you will do some research and find two articles that provide information about famous artists who carved monuments in the side of mountains.

After you have reviewed these sources, you will answer some questions about them. Briefly scan the sources and the three questions that follow. Then go back and read the sources carefully to gain the information you will need to answer the questions and finalize your research. You may take notes on the information you find in the sources as you read. Your notes will be available to you as you answer the questions.

Directions for Part 1

You will now examine several sources. You can re-examine any of the sources as often as you like.

Research Questions:

After examining the sources, use the remaining time in Part 1 to answer three questions about them. Your answers to these questions will be scored. Also, your answers will help you think about the research sources you have read and viewed, which should help you write your story. You may look at your notes when you think it would be helpful.

GO ON →

Source #1: The Making of a Monument

The idea of a mountain monument began as a way to attract tourists. According to the United States Department of the Interior, in 1923 Doane Robinson suggested that South Dakota create giant statues of explorers and Native American leaders in the Black Hills. Robinson wanted lots of visitors to come and spend their money at the businesses in his state.

An Artist's Vision

Robinson contacted the well-known artist Gutzon Borglum. Borglum read Robinson's letter with keen interest; the thought of constructing enormous stone figures fascinated him.

Before long, Borglum visited Robinson and toured the Black Hills. However, he did not care for the needle-like peaks that Robinson suggested for the statues. Borglum thought the tall spires would look like carved totem poles. Instead, Mount Rushmore offered a solid granite wall; it was the perfect carving block.

Borglum also selected his own figures to carve. He chose presidents who had notably shaped the nation's history. The foremost position would go to George Washington; people considered the first president to be the "Father of the Nation." Next on Borglum's list was Thomas Jefferson. Jefferson was responsible for much of our country's growth because he signed the Louisiana Purchase. This agreement bought American land from France, which then owned a large section of our country. Borglum chose Lincoln, too. Lincoln held the country together during the Civil War. For the last position, Borglum decided upon Theodore Roosevelt. This president built our navy and strengthened our country's powers. In addition, Roosevelt was his personal friend.

Finding Funding

Before the project began, a committee formed to find funding. While some people donated money, the amount was too little. Fortunately, Borglum persuaded President Coolidge to visit Mount Rushmore and explained his plan to him. Coolidge approved. As a result, the government agreed to pay most of the costs for workers, supplies, and tools.

GO ON →

Following a Model

How does someone begin chiseling a 60-foot-high head into a granite mountain? First, Borglum built a plaster model of the presidents. Using his model, he measured key distances, such as the width of an eye. Then he multiplied each inch by 12 feet. For instance, a one-inch eye on the model equaled a 12-foot eye on the mountain. Next, workers strapped themselves onto board-like *bosun* chairs. Carefully, ropes lowered the chairs and workers into the correct position on the cliff's face. Then the workers marked the important measurements with red paint.

Dynamite and Jackhammers

Using the paint for guidance, Borglum directed the workers to put charges of dynamite in the places where he wanted some stone removed. Amazingly, he was an expert at determining how much explosive to use to blast away certain areas. After the blasting, ropes lowered drillers with jackhammers. They made lots of shallow holes very close together in the top layer of rock. This "honeycombing" process weakened the rock, so they could take off smaller amounts by hand. Finally, workers used a spinning tool to polish the surface. The different jobs were dangerous, but the National Park Service reports no one was ever seriously injured. After 14 years, the one million dollar project was completed.

A Popular Wonder

Today, nearly three million people visit Mount Rushmore every year. However, the statues are much more than a tourist attraction. People who proudly view the presidential monument consider it to be a lasting memorial to our nation.

NPS Photo

GO ON →

Source #2: A Story Told in Stone

Some Sioux chiefs met and discussed an important idea. They wanted everyone to know their people had "great heroes." They decided to create a statue that would be a lasting symbol of their people's spirit.

Honoring a Warrior and a People

One chief, Henry Standing Bear, wrote a letter to the sculptor, Korczak Ziolkowski. The sculptor's artwork had won a prize at the World Fair and impressed him. Standing Bear asked him if he would construct a large sculpture of their brave Native American leader Crazy Horse on Thunderhead Mountain. Crazy Horse had fought for his people's rights and tried to preserve their way of life. The chiefs felt his courage and bravery represented the Sioux people well.

One Man's Mission

Ziolkowski agreed to the request. He arrived in the Black Hills in 1947 and met Standing Bear. The sculptor suggested carving Crazy Horse riding his horse with his arm extended. His finger would point at the lands where his people once lived. He wanted his masterpiece to relate the story of the Sioux nation.

To pay for the project, Ziolkowski collected donations. While the government offered grants, he turned them down. He did not believe the government would provide enough money to complete the project, and he feared government control of his work.

Carving Thunderhead Mountain

After creating a model, Ziolkowski next determined how to fit his design into Thunderhead Mountain. He began his carving with an explosion that blasted away ten tons of rock. He marked key points and used dynamite to remove unwanted stone.

However, Ziolkowski's work progressed very slowly. The large size of the statue required removing large amounts of rock. In addition, the mountain's high iron content made carving difficult. Also, at first, he had little money to pay for workers and depended on volunteers for help. Despite the challenges, he worked on the project until his death at age 74.

GO ON →

Modern Methods

Today, Ziolkowski's son is the foreman of the operation. The completed face of the Sioux warrior now gazing from Thunderhead Mountain measures nearly 90 feet. Following the sculptor's model, crews have spent the last ten years blocking out the horse's head, which will measure 220 feet.

Over time, carving methods have greatly improved. Workers now use laser beams, which reflect off the rock, to provide measurements. Special gel explosives allow accurate blasting, and bulldozers and trucks haul stone from the mountain. Jet torches polish finished surfaces.

Fortunately, the Crazy Horse Memorial Foundation is able to pay for the ongoing work on the expensive, multi-million dollar statue. The Foundation collects both donations and visitor's fees.

More Than a Memorial

While the developing sculpture attracts the most attention, the Crazy Horse Memorial offers much more. The site is the home of the Indian Museum of North America. Ziolkowski began the museum because he wanted to preserve the Native American past and tell their complete story. The Indian University of North America shares the location, too.

One day, the Crazy Horse Memorial will be the largest sculpture in the world. The proposed height is 563 feet, which is taller than the Great Pyramid. Often, people question when the sculpture will be completed, but the workers are patient. They remember that Ziolkowski always said, "Go slowly, so you do it right."

GO ON →

1 Check the box that indicates whether the information in Source #1, Source #2, or both sources supports each idea. Place a check in the Select only **one** box for **each** idea.

	Source #1: The Making of a Monument	Source #2: A Story Told in Stone	Both Sources
Wanted little government control or funding	☐	☐	☐
Federal government was heavily involved in the project	☐	☐	☐
Monument is important part of this nation's history	☐	☐	☐

2 Both sources discuss methods for carving a statue into a mountain. What does Source #1 explain about these methods that Source #2 does not? Explain why that information is helpful for the reader. Give **two** details from Source #1 to support your explanation.

_____

_____

_____

_____

_____

GO ON →

3 Each source explains that the artist wanted his memorial to give a message to those who viewed it. Explain how including this message affected the design of the monuments. Use **one** example from **each** source to support your explanation. For each example, include the source title or number.

_____

_____

_____

_____

_____

_____

Directions for Part 2

You will now review your notes and sources, and plan, draft, revise, and edit your story. You may use your notes and refer to the sources. Now read your assignment and the information about how your story will be scored; then begin your work.

Your Assignment:

Your school is having its annual writing contest. This year, the topic is about an imaginary monument being built to honor a local hero. The audience for your story is your principal, and the school board, as well as people in the community. The winning entry will be published in the local paper.

Now you are going to write a story to submit to the principal. For your story, imagine that you are the person who will be creating a monument about a young boy who helped an elderly neighbor. In your story, describe what makes the boy a hero. Then describe what happens as you plan out your design and build it. What are some important decisions you must make? The story should be several paragraphs long.

Writers often do research to add realistic details to the setting, characters, and plot in their stories. When writing your story, find ways to use information and details from the sources to improve your story. Make sure you develop your characters, the setting, and the plot. Use details, dialogue, and description where appropriate.

REMEMBER: A well-written story
- is well-organized and stays on topic
- has an introduction and conclusion
- uses details from the sources
- develops ideas fully
- uses clear language
- follows rules of writing (spelling, punctuation, and grammar)

Now begin work on your story. Manage your time carefully so that you can plan, write, revise, and edit the final draft of your story. Write your response on a separate sheet of paper.

Answer Key

Name: _____

Question	Correct Answer	Content Focus	CCSS	Complexity
1	A, F	Idioms	L.5.5b	DOK 2
2	B	Greek and Latin Prefixes	L.5.4b	DOK 2
3A	C	Context Clues: Sentence Clues	L.5.4a	DOK 2
3B	D	Context Clues: Sentence Clues/Text Evidence	L.5.4a/ RL.5.1	DOK 2
4A	A	Character, Setting, Plot: Sequence	RL.3.3	DOK 2
4B	B	Character, Setting, Plot: Sequence/ Text Evidence	RL.3.3/ RL.5.1	DOK 2
5A	C	Character, Setting, Plot: Problem and Solution	RL.4.3	DOK 2
5B	B	Character, Setting, Plot: Problem and Solution/Text Evidence	RL.4.3/ RL.5.1	DOK 2
6A	A	Character, Setting, Plot: Problem and Solution	RL.4.3	DOK 2
6B	C	Character, Setting, Plot: Problem and Solution/Text Evidence	RL.4.3/ RL.5.1	DOK 2
7	see below	Character, Setting, Plot: Problem and Solution	RL.4.3	DOK 3
8	D	Context Clues: Sentence Clues	L.5.4a	DOK 2
9	see below	Text Structure: Cause and Effect	RI.5.3	DOK 3
10	D	Context Clues: Sentence Clues	L.5.4a	DOK 2
11	A, E	Idioms	L.5.5b	DOK 2
12A	A	Text Structure: Cause and Effect	RI.5.3	DOK 2
12B	B	Text Structure: Cause and Effect/Text Evidence	RI.5.3/ RI.5.1	DOK 2
13A	B	Author's Point of View	RI.5.8	DOK 2
13B	D, F	Author's Point of View/Text Evidence	RI.5.8/ RI.5.1	DOK 2
14A	D	Author's Point of View	RI.5.8	DOK 2
14B	B	Author's Point of View/Text Evidence	RI.5.8/ RI.5.1	DOK 2
15	D	Text Structure: Cause and Effect	RI.5.5	DOK 3
16	see below	Author's Point of View	RI.5.8	DOK 3
17	C	Greek Roots	L.5.4b	DOK 2
18A	A	Idioms	L.5.4b	DOK 2
18B	D	Idioms/Text Evidence	L.5.4b/ RI.5.1	DOK 2
19	see below	Text Structure: Cause and Effect	RI.5.5	DOK 3
20	see below	Author's Point of View	RI.5.8	DOK 3
21	see below	Compare Across Texts	RI.5.9	DOK 3

Question	Correct Answer	Content Focus	CCSS	Complexity
22	A	Run-on Sentences and Fragments	L.4.1f	DOK 1
23	C	Sentences	L.4.2a	DOK 1
24	C	Sentences	L.5.1a	DOK 1
25	A	Run-on Sentences and Fragments	L.4.1f	DOK 1
26	A	Subjects and Predicates	L.5.1	DOK 1
27	D	Complex Sentences	L.5.2b	DOK 1
28	D	Compound Sentences and Conjunctions	L.5.1a	DOK 1
29	B	Subjects and Predicates	L.5.1	DOK 1
30	B	Compound Sentences and Conjunctions	L.5.1a	DOK 1
31	D	Complex Sentences	L.5.2b	DOK 1

Comprehension: Selected Response 4A, 4B, 5A, 5B, 6A, 6B, 12A, 12B, 13A, 13B, 14A, 14B, 15, 19	/16	%
Comprehension: Constructed Response 7, 9, 16, 20, 21	/12	%
Vocabulary 1, 2, 3A, 3B, 8, 10A, 10B, 11, 17, 18A, 18B	/16	%
English Language Conventions 22–31	/10	%
Total Unit Assessment Score	/54	%

7 **2-point response:** Brian's parents smile because, before the camping trip, Brian would have stopped talking to them and responded to the text right away. His parents probably are happy that the camping trip helped Brian develop a little more appreciation for nature and learn that getting away from computers and talking with his family about an interesting subject can be enjoyable and important.

9 **2-point response:** Elizabeth's father made sure that Elizabeth and her siblings had tutors in "challenging subjects like mathematics and Latin." When the family moved from England to America, Elizabeth's studies continued in an "excellent school." Her father's belief that women should have a "wide education" helped prepare Elizabeth to become a doctor.

16 **2-point response:** The author believes that it was natural for traders to choose the fastest type of transportation because their goal was to beat their competitors. Steamships were a better choice than wind-powered vessels because they were not dependent on wind or good weather.

19 Students should match the following:
- "One observer . . . ": to explain why the steamboat seemed dangerous
- "Land travel . . . ": to explain why Fulton's business grew

20 **2-point response:** Fulton's steam-powered boat did not look like other ships, and people made fun of it. Some even "thought it was a monster racing down the river." But people soon learned to appreciate its speed, and "Fulton's Folly" led to the economic success of later steamboats.

21 **4-point response:** Both the clipper ship and the steamboat could carry cargo and passengers more quickly and efficiently than older types of ships. Traditional sailing ships often took as long as 200 days to travel from New York to California, but clipper ships could cover the same distance in about half the time. Because they moved quickly, clipper ships were used to transport goods all around the world. Steamships offered luxury, even faster travel, and independence from relying on the wind to propel them. Tired of slow, unpredictable methods of transportation, people began to favor steamship travel. They also enjoyed the affordability and comfort that steamships offered.

Narrative Performance Task

Question	Answer	CCSS	Complexity	Score
1	see below	RI.5.1, RI.5.2, RI.5.7, RI.5.8, RI.5.9 W.5.2, W.5.3a-e, W.5.4, W.5.7 L.5.1, L.5.2	DOK 2	/1
2	see below		DOK 3	/2
3	see below		DOK 3	/2
Story	see below		DOK 4	/4 [P/O] /4 [D/E] /2 [C]
Total Score				**/15**

1 Students should match the following:
• Source #1: Federal government was heavily involved . . .
• Source #2: Wanted little government control . . .
• Both: Monument is important part . . .

2 **2-point response:** Source #1 tells how the measurements of the model are used to figure out the size of the statue. For example, "a one-inch eye on the model equaled a 12-foot eye on the mountain." The author also explains how the workers were lowered in chairs into position to do their jobs. "Carefully, ropes lowered the chairs and workers into the correct position on the cliff's face." These details help the reader better understand why a model is a necessary part of the sculpture process. The details about the workers help the reader better understand the dangers of the carving process.

3 **2-point response:** The artists chose certain subjects for their design or positioned them in certain ways to convey their messages. In "The Making of a Monument," Borglum wanted the memorial to tell about America's history, so he carved "presidents who had notably shaped the nation's history," like George Washington, the "Father of the Nation." In "A Story Told in Stone," Ziolkowski wanted his statue to tell the story of the Sioux nation. He carved Crazy Horse so "his finger would point at the lands where his people once lived" to show the lands that were important to the Sioux.

10-point anchor paper: My hands shook with excitement as I stood in my kitchen and read the letter from the mayor. I couldn't wait to start the job. Already, a million ideas bubbled through my mind. I called immediately to accept the challenge.

"I'm glad you're willing to do this, Abel," the mayor told me. "I have some workers lined up to help you, too, and a studio. Everything is waiting for you at Block Mountain, a small granite mountain at the edge of town. You should be able to make a spectacular statue on it."

The next morning, I set out for the mountain. Just the name of the mountain gave me inspiration. As I traveled, I thought about Billy, a young boy who had rescued an elderly neighbor, Mrs. Williams, from her burning house. I thought about how brave he must be, and what an amazing accomplishment that was. I also remembered how the famous artist Ziolkowski had decided to carve the statue of Crazy Horse pointing over the Black Hills. The statue showed how the land was special to the Sioux people, and the shape of it fit the mountain well. I had to think of a design that would fit into a rectangular-shaped block, and my statue had to tell the story of Billy's bravery.

When I arrived at Block Mountain, a man named Davis met me. He was six feet tall, with curly black hair and a beard as a big as a bush. His voice boomed like thunder as he greeted me.

"I can't wait to start blasting the rock away!" Davis laughed as he grabbed my suitcases and hurried toward the door. He had more energy than an Olympic racer.

Next, we drove to an art studio at the base of the mountain. This was where I could build my model.

"You could carve a statue of just Billy himself," Davis suggested. He recited his ideas in his booming voice until my ears rang. However, I already had my own plan.

The next morning, I got to work early in the studio, while it was empty and quiet. I used clay to build my model. I had decided to use a scale where one inch on my model would equal one foot on the mountain. That would make it easy to transfer my design to the mountain.

Quietly, I shaped my clay. After lots of thinking, I had decided to carve a statue of Billy carrying Mrs. Williams to safety, with a burning building in the background.

A week later, I completed my model. Davis had visited me every day and offered his suggestions. Sometimes, I used some of his ideas. For instance, he had told me to make the base of the statue thicker, so the rock would be sturdier. At last, we were ready to start.

First, I gave Davis the key measurements for Billy holding Mrs. Williams. They were 30 inches long and 12 inches high. Davis and his workers used ropes and bosun chairs to lower themselves into the right position on the front of the rocky cliff. They used laser beams to measure the points and mark them with bright red paint. They ended up being 30 feet long and 12 feet high. After that outline was drawn, they did the same thing for the house. When they finished, I carefully examined them. I studied and decided exactly what unwanted stone would have to be blasted away.

The next morning, Davis and his workers started using gel explosives to get rid of the unwanted stone. A bulldozer and truck waited nearby to haul away the rubble and make our job a little easier. Everything was going smoothly until the last blast. A huge lump of stone was left on top of the house.

"We can take care of that tomorrow," Davis reassured me. "That part of the stone had lots of iron in it; we need to use more explosives."

That night, as I slept, I dreamt about the lump of stone. The next morning, I searched for Davis before he could blast it away. "It's the perfect size for flames," I told him. "I'm going to add it to my design!"

For the next several months, I directed the work on the carvings. The men used modern drills to shape the next layer. They "honeycombed" the rock by drilling many holes close together, and then they removed smaller pieces of rock with their hands. It was exciting to see my design emerging from the stone. Finally, it was time for the men to polish the stone with their jet torches.

Before school started in September, the mayor came to see the completed masterpiece; he was very pleased with the work. A celebration was held, and the public was invited to view the statue.

"Now I have a favor I would like you to do for me," I boldly told the mayor as the people began to leave. "You should have a museum built about heroes at this location. Then people can learn even more about people who have helped others."

"That's an excellent idea," the mayor agreed with a slow smile.

"Davis is the perfect person for the job," I added. If the Mayor put Davis in charge, the museum might be done in day!

Read the text. Then answer the questions.

The Prince Who Learned Wisdom

There once lived a prince who would someday become the ruler. "Study hard, my boy," his father advised him. "You will require an excellent education when you are crowned king."

The prince took these words to heart and studied hard every day, until one day, a thought came to him. "My teachers give me a lot of useful knowledge, but I wonder if I am gaining the wisdom that a ruler needs." He decided the answer was no. To gain wisdom, he would require a new plan.

The prince informed his father that he wanted to visit a nearby country whose philosophers were said to be very wise. He would ask them to teach him their wisdom. The king considered this idea to be very foolish. "Wisdom comes only from a good education," he declared firmly. "Your teachers are preparing you very well." Still, he agreed to let his son go, even giving the young man some gold coins for his journey. Neither suspected that the prince's search would end up taking him in a very different direction.

Early the next morning, the prince set out. To avoid attracting attention, he dressed in ordinary clothes and carried his belongings on his back like anyone else. As he strode along, he whistled a cheerful tune, happy to be travelling on his own.

By afternoon, his stomach was growling loudly, so he sat down in a nearby field to eat his lunch. The warm sun stroking his cheek and the soft breeze whispering in his ears made him drowsy.

The prince was awakened suddenly by the crackling of dry leaves. A thief was scurrying away with his pack! He was too far away to catch, so the prince was forced to go on without it. (Luckily, the gold coins were hidden safely inside his coat.) He continued on, pondering what had occurred. As he was thinking deeply, he came to a realization. "Anything can happen when you sleep outside. When I become the ruler, I must make sure that everyone in my kingdom has a safe place to sleep."

Then he laughed. "That fellow actually gave me a bit of wisdom!"

GO ON →

As evening approached, it began to rain heavily. With a great distance remaining and his feet soggy, the prince stopped at an inn. Aching with hunger, he welcomed the scents of fresh bread and savory stew that met him at the door. After a hearty, delicious meal, he climbed the stairs to his room, blew out the candle, and crawled peacefully into bed-but not for long. *CREEEEEAK!* A young woman tiptoed into the shadowy room and quietly picked up the prince's boots. As she tried to creep out again, the prince leaped up, blocked her way, and yelled for the innkeeper. When the man arrived, the outraged prince informed him that the woman had been stealing his boots.

"No, she wasn't," the innkeeper replied, shaking his head vigorously. "She was taking them downstairs to the fire so they would dry before morning. I'm sorry if my daughter disturbed you."

Feeling embarrassed, the prince quickly gave the daughter a gold coin as an apology. Back in bed, he reflected over what had happened. "When I am king, I must be sure to get all the facts before I make a judgment," he concluded. Then, laughing, "I never expected to acquire wisdom in a village inn!"

The following day, instead of continuing on, the prince returned the way he had come. He did not stop until he was inside the palace.

"Back already?" exclaimed his father. "You can't possibly have made it even to the border. Why did you give up your plan?"

"Father," replied the prince earnestly, "in just two days, I gained enough wisdom to know that it was not the most advantageous plan. I now realize there is no need to seek wisdom in distant places. I have learned that wisdom can in fact be discovered anywhere by simply paying attention and learning from personal experiences." Hearing this response, the king smiled and nodded with satisfaction at his young son.

From that day forward, the prince made a point of leaving the palace at least twice a week to observe and listen to what was happening among the people. When the time came for him to become king, he was a very wise ruler indeed.

GO ON →

1 Read the sentences from the text.

By afternoon, his stomach was growling loudly, so he sat down in a nearby field to eat his lunch. The warm sun stroking his cheek and the soft breeze whispering in his ears made him drowsy.

What does the phrase "warm sun stroking his cheek and the soft breeze whispering in his ears" mean?

(A) Someone was touching the prince's head while he was sleeping.

(B) The sun and breeze were especially strong that afternoon.

(C) The sun and breeze were both like a gentle person.

(D) The prince was not used to sleeping outside.

2 The following question has two parts. First, answer part A. Then, answer part B.

Part A: Read the sentences from the text.

He continued on, pondering what had occurred. As he was thinking deeply, he came to a realization.

What does the word pondering **most likely** mean?

(A) trying to understand

(B) feeling motivated by

(C) trying to escape from

(D) feeling embarrassed by

Part B: Which detail from the sentences provides the **best** clue to the meaning of the word pondering?

(A) "continued on"

(B) "had occurred"

(C) "thinking deeply"

(D) "a realization"

GO ON →

3 What is the purpose of the illustration in the text?

(A) to show how the prince's pack was stolen

(B) to explain why the thief wanted the prince's pack

(C) to describe how the prince felt about being robbed

(D) to indicate where the prince's gold coins were hidden

4 How are the thief and the innkeeper's daughter alike?

(A) Both try to steal something from the prince.

(B) Both end up with gold belonging to the prince.

(C) Both wake up the prince by accidentally touching him.

(D) Both teach the prince a lesson without knowing it.

Name: _____ Date: _____

5 Read the sentence from the text.

"Father," replied the prince earnestly, "in just two days, I gained enough wisdom to know that it was not the most <u>advantageous</u> plan.

If the suffix *-ous* means "full of or having," what does <u>advantageous</u> mean? Select **two** options.

(A) exciting

(B) beneficial

(C) unprofitable

(D) helpful

(E) terrifying

(F) powerful

6 The following question has two parts. First, answer part A. Then, answer part B.

Part A: Which sentence **best** states the theme of the text?

(A) A wise person thinks before speaking.

(B) Do not be afraid to give up on foolish ideas.

(C) Lessons can be learned in unexpected ways.

(D) Treat others the way you want to be treated.

Part B: Which sentence from the text **best** supports your answer in Part A?

(A) "To avoid attracting attention, he dressed in ordinary clothes and carried his belongings on his back like anyone else."

(B) "'When I am king, I must be sure to get all the facts before I make a judgment,' he concluded."

(C) "The following day, instead of continuing on, the prince returned the way he had come."

(D) "'I have learned that wisdom can in fact be discovered anywhere by simply paying attention and learning from personal experiences.'"

GO ON →

7 Read the sentence from the text.

Neither suspected that the prince's search would end up taking him in a very different direction.

Why did the author include this sentence near the beginning of the text? Support your answer with details from the text.

_____

_____

_____

_____

_____

Read the text. Then answer the questions.

Maureen Connolly: Tennis Star!

"I think that I could keep on playing even if they set off dynamite in the middle of the court," said Maureen Connolly, a tennis player who won tennis championships in four countries when she was only 19 years old. Many people think that Maureen Connolly was the best female tennis star who ever played.

Maureen Connolly was born in San Diego, California, in 1934. She loved riding horses as a little girl, but her mother could not pay for riding lessons. She asked Maureen to find a less expensive hobby. Maureen decided she wanted to play tennis.

Maureen was very ambitious. That is, she was determined to do whatever it took to achieve her goals. She paid for her first tennis lessons by picking up tennis balls at the tennis courts. She worked hard and won her first tennis tournament just a few months later. After that taste of victory, Maureen had found the sport she loved. She dedicated three hours a day to tennis.

Maureen, who was only 5'4" and 120 pounds, needed a special tennis racket because her hands were so small. But Maureen proved that small players could be powerful too. At age 14 she won 56 tennis matches in a row! She then became the youngest girl to win the Female Under 18 United States Championship. Fans found Maureen irresistible and loved watching her play. She spent lots of time signing her name on photos when people asked for her autograph. When people started calling her "Little Mo," she went along with it. After all, "Big Mo" was a famous battleship of that time, strong and powerful.

When Maureen was 16 years old, she became the youngest female ever to win the U.S. Open, the biggest tennis tournament in the country. One sports reporter called her a "killer on the courts" because of the way she hit the ball. In 1953, Maureen won the four biggest tennis tournaments in the world. She won the championships in Australia, England, the United States, and France.

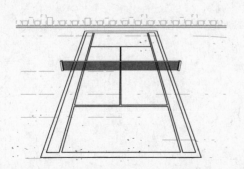 

GO ON →

Maureen was also the youngest female player ever to win the Wimbledon tournament in England. By the age of 20, she was the number one female tennis player in the world. She was also named the Associated Press Woman Athlete of the Year for three years in a row. Then, in 1954, just a few weeks after winning her third Wimbledon tournament, Maureen was in a terrible accident. She was hit by a truck while horseback riding. One of her legs was badly crushed. Maureen then turned her powers to getting well. She tried to play tennis again, but the damage to her leg was too severe. At the age of 20, "Little Mo" retired from tennis.

Yet real champions go on winning in other ways. Soon, she began writing a sports column for a local newspaper. She also taught tennis to children and teenagers. Maureen and her husband, Norman Brinker, wanted to found a group that would help create tennis programs for young players. To do so, they started the Maureen Connolly Brinker Foundation.

Maureen died from cancer at only 34 years old. But in her short life, she enjoyed much success.

GO ON →

8 Read the sentences from the text.

Maureen was very <u>ambitious</u>. That is, she was determined to do whatever it took to achieve her goals.

What does <u>ambitious</u> mean?

(A) greedy

(B) skillful

(C) eager for success

(D) annoying to others

9 Maureen's mother did not have enough money to pay for riding lessons. How did Maureen overcome this problem? Support your answer with details from the text.

_____

_____

_____

_____

_____

GO ON →

10 Read the sentence from the text.

One sports reporter called her a killer on the courts.

Why did the reporter describe Maureen Connolly with the phrase "killer on the courts"?

(A) She tried to hurt other players.

(B) She was injured frequently.

(C) She was rude to reporters.

(D) She hit the ball with a lot of power.

11 Read the sentence from the text.

Maureen and her husband, Norman Brinker, wanted to <u>found</u> a group that would help create tennis programs for young players.

Which answers define the word <u>found</u> as it is used in the sentence? Select **two** options.

(A) locate

(B) organize

(C) furnish

(D) establish

(E) take over

(F) search for

GO ON →

12 The following question has two parts. First, answer part A. Then, answer part B.

Part A: How does the author organize this article?

(A) by describing events in the order in which they happened

(B) by stating a problem and showing how Maureen solved it

(C) by comparing Maureen's early life to her tennis-playing years

(D) by describing different situations and telling what caused each one

Part B: Which sentences from the text **best** support your answer in part A? Select **two** options.

(A) "Many people think that Maureen Connolly was the best female tennis star who ever played."

(B) "She loved riding horses as a little girl, but her mother could not pay for riding lessons."

(C) "She then became the youngest girl to win the Female Under 18 United States Championship."

(D) "After all, "Big Mo" was a famous battleship of that time, strong and powerful."

(E) "In 1953, Maureen won the four biggest tennis tournaments in the world."

(F) "But in her short life, she enjoyed much success."

GO ON →

Name: _____ Date: _____

13 Select the **four** most important events in Maureen's life and number them in the order in which they occurred.

_____ She was in a horrible accident.

_____ She was given a special nickname.

_____ She had to stop taking horse riding lessons.

_____ She won her third Wimbledon tournament.

_____ She had a special tennis racket made.

_____ She began giving tennis lessons.

14 Which sentences from the text **best** support the idea that Maureen did not let obstacles stop her from achieving her goals? Select **all** that apply.

(A) "She paid for her first tennis lessons by picking up tennis balls at the tennis courts."

(B) "She spent lots of time signing her name on photos when people asked for her autograph."

(C) "Maureen, who was only 5'4" and 120 pounds, needed a special tennis racket because her hands were so small."

(D) "When people started calling her 'Little Mo,' she went along with it."

(E) "She was hit by a truck while horseback riding."

(F) "Soon, she began writing a sports column for a local newspaper."

GO ON →

Read the texts. Then answer the questions.

How Green Is Greensburg?

A few years ago, not many people outside of Kansas had ever heard of the little town of Greensburg (population 1,500). Its main claim to fame was a tourist attraction, the World's Largest Hand-Dug Well. Today, however, the town is known world-wide. Given the town's name, it is fitting that its fame now comes from being "green."

May 4, 2007
Residents of Greensburg didn't consider the potential danger ahead when the weather reports predicted thunderstorms. That doesn't mean residents don't take twisters seriously. When alarm sirens told them that a tornado had actually been spotted nearby, they moved quickly into basements and storm shelters.

At 9:45 p.m., the tornado crashed into Greensburg. It measured about 1.7 miles across, nearly as wide as the entire town. Its swirling winds were moving at more than 200 miles per hour. Like a gigantic, out-of-control bulldozer, the tornado zigzagged through Greensburg. When it finally moved on, it had demolished about 95 percent of the town. Homes, businesses, schools, churches, the hospital—even the trees, all destroyed or badly damaged. The electricity was out, and water supplies could not be trusted. Even worse, ten people had been killed.

Time Line for Greensburg Tornado

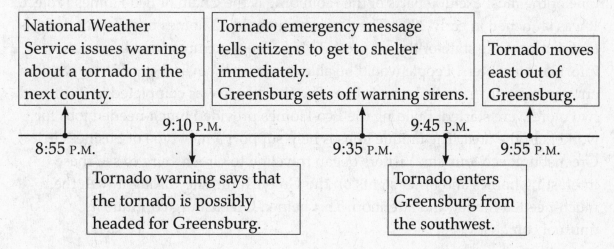

GO ON →

Planning a New Direction

Less than a week after the tornado, the community made the decision that would change Greensburg forever. The people decided that they would rebuild the town green—that is, in ways that were good for the environment. City buildings would use eco-friendly materials and be energy efficient. Citizens would build new homes the same way. Electricity would come from alternative energy sources, such as the wind and sun. Instead of giving up on Greensburg, people got excited about its future.

Building a New Town

Greensburg moved ahead quickly. The first challenge, however, was just keeping the town going. Government helped provide services and housing. A temporary hospital, school, and city-hall were set up.

In October 2009, Greensburg started constructing a wind farm with giant windmills. The wind farm would supply energy for the town. The new county hospital that opened in March 2010 was built to strict LEED standards. (LEED stands for a program called Leadership in Energy and Environmental Design. Its purpose is to support green construction.) The town hall, courthouse, and arts center are also LEED buildings. The new school for grades K through 12 was finished in August 2010. It has natural daytime lighting and other energy-efficient features. Nearly half the homes in town were rebuilt according to green guidelines. Even the streetlights are designed to use less energy and reduce nighttime light pollution.

One of the most exciting parts of the rebuilding is the Chain of Eco-Homes Project. It was launched in early 2009. The plan was to build 12 homes in different designs that demonstrate state-of-the-art green living. The structures would serve as information centers. People would be able to stay in them and experience what an environmentally-friendly home is like. The first house was completed in 2010, and two more were started. Building the Eco-Homes provided much-needed jobs for workers in the area. The unique houses help support a new type of business in Greensburg: eco-tourism. Visitors began traveling to Greensburg to see these interesting homes and other sights on the Green Tour. They brought with them much-needed money and attention. This helped Greensburg continue its unusual comeback.

GO ON →

Chicago, Reborn

On October 8, 1871, the great city of Chicago, Illinois, was destroyed by a massive fire. Many people believe the fire was started by a cow in a local barn. While the exact cause is unknown, the tragedy changed the city forever. Chicago was the second most populated city in America at the time of the fire. Since the entire business district was destroyed in the blaze, rebuilding was quite a task. The townspeople needed leadership, direction, and inspiration so that all hope would not be lost.

Keeping the Faith

Initially, the people of Chicago were in shock. However, in the days that followed, their determination was shown. New businesses began to spring up all over the city. Rubble from the fire was cleared away. Large amounts were dumped into the lake, creating new areas to rebuild on. Important services like grocery stores, and post offices were moved to buildings left standing.

One brave and inspiring Chicagoan was William D. Kerfoot. William bought and sold houses and business property in Chicago before the fire struck. The day after the fire ended, William went to the location where his office once stood and saw that it was completely destroyed. He could have lost hope and gone home. Instead, he reopened his business by simply setting up a few temporary walls on the pile where his office used to be. He did not believe in quitting and posted a sign that read: "All gone but WIFE CHILDREN and ENERGY". This showed that he was going to persevere no matter what, and inspired other business owners to do the same.

There was also a need for new leadership. The citizens of Chicago elected Joseph Medill as their new mayor within a month of the fire. He promised to make sure the city followed new and improved building and fire codes. The codes required new buildings to be built using fireproof materials, like brick. He also promised that the rebuilding of the city was his main focus. The people of Chicago needed someone to believe in and follow at this time. They wanted someone who they could believe would protect them from letting this happen again.

The Plan Comes Together

Thanks to the leadership and inspiration of the people of Chicago, not only was the city rebuilt, it became better than it ever was before. The effort to rebuild Chicago created many job opportunities and helped the economy grow. The population also grew as people came to the area searching for open jobs. With a clean slate to start with, architects were able to build a safer and more modernized city, including the opportunity to build some of the world's first skyscrapers.

GO ON →

Answer these questions about "How Green Is Greenburg?"

15 The following question has two parts. First, answer part A. Then, answer part B.

Part A: Read the sentences from "How Green Is Greensburg?"

When it finally moved on, it had <u>demolished</u> about 95 percent of the town. Homes, businesses, schools, churches, the hospital, even the trees—all destroyed or badly damaged.

What does <u>demolished</u> mean in the sentences above?

(A) avoided

(B) wrecked

(C) missed

(D) involved

Part B: Which phrase from the sentences helps the reader understand the meaning of the word <u>demolished</u>?

(A) "finally moved on"

(B) "about 95 percent of the town"

(C) "even the trees"

(D) "destroyed or badly damaged"

GO ON →

16 What information does the time line provide about the night of May 4, 2007, and what the people of Greensburg experienced? Use details from the text to support your answer.

_____

_____

_____

_____

_____

17 Which statement **best** describes how Greensburg recovered from the tornado?

(A) It doubled its population.

(B) It secured itself against future tornadoes.

(C) It became an eco-tourism destination.

(D) It began the Chain of Eco-Homes Project.

GO ON →

Name: _____ Date: _____

Answer these questions about "Chicago, Reborn."

18 The following question has two parts. First, answer part A. Then, answer part B.

Part A: Read the sentences from the text.

He did not believe in quitting and posted a sign that read: "All gone but WIFE CHILDREN and ENERGY". This showed that he was going to persevere no matter what, and inspired other business owners to do the same.

What is **most likely** the meaning of the word persevere as it is used in the sentence?

(A) move away

(B) keep going

(C) create change

(D) protect others

Part B: Which phrase from the sentences **best** supports your answer in part A?

(A) "did not believe in quitting"

(B) "posted a sign"

(C) "inspired other business owners"

(D) "do the same"

GO ON →

60

Copyright © McGraw-Hill Education

19 Why did the author include the information about the new buildings in Chicago being built out of brick? Support your answer with details from the text.

_____

_____

_____

_____

_____

_____

20 How does the author help the reader understand the information in the text?

(A) by including the dates when they took place

(B) by arranging events in the order they occurred

(C) by using words such as "first," "next," and "last"

(D) by showing how one event resulted from another

GO ON →

Now answer this question about "How Green Is Greensburg?" and "Chicago, Reborn."

21 With determination and hard work, people can overcome difficult challenges. How do the people of Greensburg, Kansas, and Chicago, Illinois, illustrate this idea? Use details from both texts to support your response.

_____

_____

_____

_____

_____

_____

_____

_____

_____

_____

_____

_____

_____

GO ON →

The text below needs revision. Read the text. Then answer the questions.

Believe it or not, doctors in the past did not wash their hands before treating patients. They did not know that diseases were spread by germs. They did not even know that germs existed.

In the mid-1800s, two doctors made important __(1)__ about preventing the spread of disease. Ignaz Semmelweis (1818–1865) of Hungary noticed that many new mothers and children were dying from infections. He showed that a lot more survived when __(2)__ and doctors cleaned their hands thoroughly. People made fun of his ideas, but Dr. Semmelweis was right.

Joseph Lister (1827–1912) was a surgeon from __(3)__. In 1865, he decided that germs caused infections. At first he thought germs only spread through the air. Then he realized that a __(4)__ hands and instruments also spread germs. After that, Lister made sure that everything in the operating room was kept very clean, including the patient.

The work of these two men has saved many __(5)__ over the years. Today, doctors and hospitals know how important it is to keep as many germs as possible away from their patients.

GO ON →

22 Which answer should go in blank (1)?

(A) discoverers

(B) discoveries

(C) discoverys

23 Which answer should go in blank (2)?

(A) nurse

(B) nurses

(C) nursies

24 Which answer should go in blank (3)?

(A) Great Britain

(B) Great britain

(C) great Britain

25 Which answer should go in blank (4)?

(A) doctors's

(B) doctor's

(C) doctors'

26 Which answer should go in blank (5)?

(A) lifes

(B) livs

(C) lives

GO ON →

The text below needs revision. Read the text. Then answer the questions.

(1) Many years ago, chipmunks did not have stripes on their backs as they do now. (2) They were a plain rusty brown all over. (3) This color made it much easier for their enemies to see them. (4) It was very dangerous being a chipmunk in those days.

(5) One morning, a cat caught a chipmunk and carried it into the kitchen. (6) When the cat's owners yelled, the startled cat dropped its prey. (7) Quickly, the chipmunk scooted away and hid behind the woodstove. (8) The peoples were cooking, and the stove was warm. (9) It burned the chipmunk's fur just a little bit. (10) By the time the chipmunk escaped, it had black, gray, and white stripes all down its back.

(11) The chipmunk found that its new colors gave it protection. (12) The stripes looked like bands of shadow and sunlight, making it much easier to hide from predators. (13) Other chipmunks decided they wanted striped coats too. (14) Soon they were finding ways to sneak into the house and visit the woodstove. (15) That's why today chipmunkses' coats all have stripes.

GO ON →

Name: _____ **Date:** _____

27 What is the prepositional phrase in sentence 1?

(A) Many years ago

(B) did not have stripes

(C) on their backs

(D) as they do now

28 What is the purpose of the prepositional phrase in sentence 7?

(A) to show how the chipmunk ran

(B) to tell where the chipmunk hid

(C) to tell where the stove was

(D) to describe the stove

29 How can sentence 8 **best** be written?

(A) The people's was cooking, and the stove was warm.

(B) The peoples' were cooking, and the stove was warm.

(C) The people was cooking, and the stove was warm.

(D) The people were cooking, and the stove was warm.

30 Which sentence contains an abstract noun?

(A) Sentence 8

(B) Sentence 10

(C) Sentence 11

(D) Sentence 13

31 How can sentence 15 **best** be written?

(A) That's why today chipmunks's coats all have stripes.

(B) That's why today chipmunks' coats all have stripes.

(C) That's why today chipmunk's coats all have stripes.

(D) That's why today chipmunks coats all have stripes.

STOP

Copyright © McGraw-Hill Education

Informational Performance Task

Task:

Your class has been learning about inventors and how they put their plans into action. Now your school newspaper is creating a special edition about inventions. Your teacher has asked you to write an informational article about the process of turning an idea into an invention. Before you begin, you do some research and find two articles that provide information about famous inventors, and one article about how to get a patent for your invention.

After you have reviewed these sources, you will answer some questions about them. Briefly scan the sources and the three questions that follow. Then go back and read the sources carefully to gain the information you will need to answer the questions and finalize your research. You may take notes on the information you find in the sources as you read. Your notes will be available to you as you answer the questions.

Directions for Part 1

You will now examine several sources. You can re-examine any of the sources as often as you like.

Research Questions:

After examining the sources, use the remaining time in Part 1 to answer three questions about them. Your answers to these questions will be scored. Also, your answers will help you think about the research sources you have read and viewed, which should help you write your informational article.

You may look at your notes when you think it would be helpful.

GO ON →

Source #1: George Nissen

When George Nissen was sixteen years old, he saw something that sparked an invention. George saw a trapeze act at the circus. The trapeze artists would twirl and swing from ropes and swings high in the air, while beneath them was a safety net. Sometimes, the trapeze artists would bounce down onto the safety net on purpose, and then do somersaults. George thought that looked like fun, especially if they could find a way to continue bouncing and performing somersaults. This sparked an idea that would take George on a life-long journey.

George was particularly interested because he enjoyed gymnastics and swimming. The nets reminded him of jumping off a diving board. He decided to take on the challenge of creating something that would allow someone to continuously bounce. In his parents' garage, George's first attempts resulted in a stretched canvas sheet inside a metal frame. Later, in college, George improved his "bouncing rig" with the help of his gymnastics teacher, Larry Griswald. This time, he used a nylon sheet which allowed for better bouncing.

George and two acrobat friends made a traveling show, called the Three Leonardos, that utilized their new bouncing rig. When they were traveling and performing in Mexico, George came up with the name trampoline. *Trampolin* means diving board in Spanish. He just added an *e*.

George thought the trampoline was wonderful. In 1942 he founded a trampoline company and spent years traveling around the world showing off what people can do on trampolines. He held competitions for rebound tumbling, the original name of trampoline competitions. He thought it would be neat if people could compete on trampolines in the Olympics. He invented games, such as Spaceball, a combination between basketball and volleyball. He even rented a kangaroo to bounce with him in Central Park. He sometimes would go to extreme lengths to promote his invention. In 1997, he performed acrobatics atop a flat-top pyramid, in Egypt.

Finally, he got his wish to see trampolines in the Olympics. In the year 2000, trampoline gymnastics became an Olympic sport. George went to watch at the Olympics that year. He was invited to try out the trampoline the athletes would use. He did. He was 86 years old.

GO ON →

Source #2: Chester Greenwood

In the town of Farmington, Maine, the first Saturday of December is Chester Greenwood Day. Residents of the town line the streets to honor a man that developed practical solutions to everyday problems. One idea that made him famous was one that he created when he was only fifteen years old.

Like many inventors, Chester had a problem to solve. Maine winters were cold. People would wrap wool scarves around their heads, but the scarves were scratchy and Chester was allergic to wool. One day, in 1873, Chester had been ice skating and was becoming frustrated because he couldn't protect his ears from the cold. Suddenly he thought of a way to keep them warm: ear muffs. He made a wire frame with two loops that would go over the ears and asked his grandmother to help him sew cloth and beaver fur to the frame.

Chester's family had a lot to do with his creativity and ambition. His father was bridge builder and businessman, and many of the children in the family were creative and mechanical like their father. He, and his siblings, always worked hard to help out around the family farm. Sometimes, Chester would travel several miles to sell fudge and candy that he made himself.

Chester Greenwood is called the inventor of ear muffs. However, he did not really invent them. Ear muffs already existed, but he found a way to make them better. While his first design was immediately popular with his friends and local children, Chester was not satisfied. Like many inventors, Chester decided to make improvements to his design. He replaced the wire with flexible steel. The new material permitted a small hinge to be attached to each ear flap that allowed them to swivel. This prevented the ear flaps from flapping around. The earmuffs could also be folded up to fit neatly in a pocket. Compared to ear muffs that are made today, Chester's ear muffs were not comfortable. However, they were an improvement on what was available at the time.

Chester called his ear muffs "Champion Ear Protectors." On March 13, 1877, he received a patent for his design. He then started a company that made and sold them. He built the company in his hometown of Farmington, Maine, which provided jobs for many people in his community.

Chester went on to invent more than a hundred things that he thought would make people's lives easier. He made a special type of teapot, a machine for working with wood, an improved rake, and many other things. Chester found creative solutions to problems, and the people of Farmington, Maine, have not forgotten him.

GO ON →

Source #3: Getting a Patent

What is a patent?

Let's say you invent something brand new. No one has ever thought of it before, but it is so useful, everyone is going to want one. How can you make and sell your invention and make sure other companies don't make it too? You can apply for a patent. This gives you the legal right to keep other people from using your idea.

What can be patented?

In order for you to patent your invention, it must be a new idea or it must be a big improvement on an old idea. Also, it should be something useful and not be completely obvious. Finally, it needs to be something that the public does not already know about. It is also important to be able to describe your invention clearly and possibly draw a picture or diagram of it. A patent applies to exactly what the inventor describes, so wording is important.

For example, it would be impossible to patent the wheel. Everyone knows about the wheel already. It is not a new idea. However, people patent special types of wheels that they invent to solve specific problems. In order to do this, they need to describe how their inventions are different from a plain wheel and from other special types of wheels. They also need to describe how their inventions work and how they are useful.

How can I find out if my idea is a new one?

Figuring out whether or not you were the first person to think of your invention may be the most difficult part of getting a patent. There are over seven million patented inventions in the United States alone. It is a good idea to search for similar inventions because you will need to show how your invention is unique. The patent office has a special system for organizing inventions to make it easier for people to do searches.

In addition, you should look through journals and books related to your invention. It is possible that someone invented something and wrote about it. Even if it is not patented, it may be considered part of public knowledge. Then, it cannot be patented.

Can I get help filing my patent?

Many people hire patent lawyers to help them research their inventions and file patents. However, this can be expensive, and it is possible to do it yourself. The people who work in the U.S. Patent Office like to help whenever they can, especially when they know someone is filing a patent without the help of a lawyer. Also, there are websites that give good advice on how to go through the process. It is possible for determined inventors to research, describe, and file patents for their inventions themselves.

GO ON →

1 Draw a line to connect **each** detail from Source #1 with **one** statement from Source #3 that supports it. Not all details will be used.

Ideas in Source #1	Details in Source #3

The earmuffs Chester patented were an improvement on what was available at the time.

"A patent applies to exactly what the inventor describes, so wording is important."

"It is a good idea to search for similar inventions because you will need to show how your invention is unique."

"They also need to describe how their inventions work and how they are useful."

Chester invented his earmuffs to solve a problem.

"However, people patent special types of wheels that they invent to solve specific problems."

"How can you make and sell your invention and make sure other companies don't make it too? You can apply for a patent."

"In order for you to patent your invention, it must be a new idea or it must be a big improvement on an old idea."

Chester started a company that made and sold his earmuffs.

GO ON →

2 Explain how the information about patents in Source #3 would be helpful if it were added to Sources #1 and #2. Use **one** example from Source #1 and **one** example from Source #2 to support your response. For each example, include the source title or number.

_____

_____

_____

_____

_____

3 Explain how an idea can develop into something that can solve a problem. Use **one** example from Source #1 and **one** example from Source #2 to support your explanation. For each example, include the source title or number.

_____

_____

_____

_____

_____

GO ON →

Directions for Part 2:

Your Assignment:

Your school newspaper is creating a special edition about inventors. Your teacher has asked you to write a multi-paragraph informational article explaining how to turn an idea into an invention. The audience for your article will be your classmates, teachers, and the principal. In your article, clearly state your main idea and support your main idea with details using information from what you have read.

Now you are going to write your article to submit to the school newspaper. Your article should include information about developing an idea for an invention. Choose the most important information from all three sources to support your ideas. Then, write an informational article that is several paragraphs long. Clearly organize your article and support your ideas with details from the sources. Use your own words except when quoting directly from the sources. Be sure to give the source title or number when using details from the sources.

REMEMBER: A well-written informational article
- has a clear main idea
- is well organized and stays on topic
- has an introduction and conclusion
- uses transitions
- uses details from the sources to support your main idea
- puts the information from the sources in your own words, except when using direct quotations from the sources
- gives the title or number of the source for the details or facts you included
- develops ideas clearly
- uses clear language
- follows rules of writing (spelling, punctuation, and grammar usage)

Now begin work on your informational article. Manage your time carefully so that you can plan, write, revise, and edit the final draft of your informational article. Write your response on a separate sheet of paper.

Question	Correct Answer	Content Focus	CCSS	Complexity
1	C	Personification	L.5.5a	DOK 2
2A	A	Context Clues: Definitions and Restatements	L.5.4a	DOK 2
2B	C	Context Clues: Definitions and Restatements/Text Evidence	L.5.4a/ RL.5.1	DOK 2
3	A	Text Features: Use Illustrations	RL.4.7	DOK 2
4	D	Character, Setting, Plot: Compare and Contrast	RL.5.3	DOK 2
5	B, D	Greek and Latin Suffixes	L.5.4b	DOK 2
6A	C	Theme	RL.5.2	DOK 2
6B	D	Theme/Text Evidence	RL.5.2/ RL.5.1	DOK 2
7	see below	Literary Elements: Foreshadowing	RL.5.1	DOK 3
8	C	Context Clues: Definitions and Restatements	L.5.4a	DOK 2
9	see below	Text Structure: Problem and Solution	RI.5.3	DOK 3
10	D	Metaphor	L.5.5a	DOK 2
11	B, D	Homographs	L.5.5c	DOK 2
12A	A	Text Structure: Sequence	RI.5.3	DOK 2
12B	C, E	Text Structure: Sequence/Text Evidence	RI.5.3/ RI.5.1	DOK 2
13	see below	Text Structure: Sequence	RI.5.3	DOK 2
14	A, C, F	Text Structure: Problem and Solution	RI.5.3	DOK 2
15A	B	Context Clues: Definitions and Restatements	L.5.4a	DOK 2
15B	D	Context Clues: Definitions and Restatements/Text Evidence	L.5.4a/ RI.5.1	DOK 2
16	see below	Text Features: Time Lines	RI.4.7	DOK 2
17	C	Text Structure: Problem and Solution	RI.5.3	DOK 2
18A	B	Context Clues: Definitions and Restatements	L.5.4a	DOK 2
18B	A	Context Clues: Definitions and Restatements/Text Evidence	L.5.4a/ RI.5.1	DOK 2
19	see below	Text Structure: Problem and Solution	RI.5.3	DOK 3
20	B	Text Structure: Sequence	RI.5.3	DOK 2

Name: _____

Question	Correct Answer	Content Focus	CCSS	Complexity
21	see below	Compare Across Texts	RI.5.9	DOK 4
22	A	Singular and Plural Nouns	L.5.2	DOK 1
23	B	Singular and Plural Nouns	L.5.2	DOK 1
24	A	Nouns	L.5.2	DOK 1
25	B	Possessive Nouns	L.5.2	DOK 1
26	C	Singular and Plural Nouns	L.5.2	DOK 1
27	C	Nouns in Prepositional Phrases	L.5.1a	DOK 1
28	B	Nouns in Prepositional Phrases	L.5.1a	DOK 1
29	D	Singular and Plural Nouns	L.5.2	DOK 1
30	C	Nouns	L.5.2	DOK 1
31	B	Possessive Nouns	L.5.2	DOK 1

Comprehension: Selected Response 3, 4, 6A, 6B, 12A, 12B, 13, 14, 17, 20	/16	%
Comprehension: Constructed Response 7, 9, 16, 19, 21	/12	%
Vocabulary 1, 2A, 2B, 5, 8, 10, 11, 15A, 15B, 18A, 18B	/16	%
English Language Conventions 22–31	/10	%
Total Unit Assessment Score	/54	%

7 **2-point response:** The author included this sentence to grab the reader's interest by giving a hint that something unexpected will happen later. The prince starts out planning to visit some philosophers but quickly changes his plans when he realizes that he can gain wisdom from everyday situations and ordinary people. This is the "different direction" that the sentence talks about. He accomplishes his goal, but not the way he expected.

9 **2-point response:** The author says that Maureen started playing tennis because she could not afford to take horseback riding lessons. She wanted a hobby, so she played tennis instead. To earn money for her tennis lessons, she picked up tennis balls for other players.

13 Students should put the events in the following order:

1: She had to stop taking horse riding lessons.
2: She won her third Wimbledon tournament.
3: She was in a horrible accident.
4: She began giving tennis lessons.

16 **2-point response:** The time line shows that the people of Greensburg received warnings of a possible tornado at 9:10 p.m. At 9:35, they realized that the tornado was approaching. They had only 10 minutes to take shelter, and the tornado destroyed almost everything in town in about 10 minutes.

19 **2-point response:** Brick is a fireproof building material. After the great fire, the city improved its building and fire codes, and the new codes required brick and other fireproof materials to be used in the construction of new buildings. This was how the city acted to prevent future destruction by fires. Because of this commitment to safety, the city of Chicago experienced job and population growth.

21 **4-point response:** The people in both towns focused on rebuilding instead of giving up. After their city was devastated by fire in the late 1800's, the people of Chicago chose to focus on what they had, rather than on what they had lost, and they decided to rebuild. They implemented new safety codes to protect the city from future fires.

When the tornado destroyed Greensburg, the townspeople could have given up and moved someplace else, or they could have rebuilt everything the same way it was before. Instead, they decided to make something new and exciting. By working together, they rebuilt Greensburg as a "green" town. Their efforts, like the efforts of the people of Chicago, resulted in safer and cleaner environments, employment opportunities, tourism, and pride in their towns.

Copyright © McGraw-Hill Education

Answer Key

Name: _____

Informational Performance Task				
Question	Answer	CCSS	Complexity	Score
1	see below	RI.5.1, RI.5.2, RI.5.7, RI.5.9, W.5.2a-e, W.5.4, W.5.7 L.5.1, L.5.2	DOK 2	/1
2	see below		DOK 3	/2
3	see below		DOK 3	/2
Informational Article	see below		DOK 4	/4 [P/O] /4 [E/E] /2 [C]
Total Score				/15

1 Students should match the following ideas and details:
- The earmuffs Chester patented…: "In order for you to patent your invention,…"
- Chester invented his earmuffs…: "However, people patent special types…"
- Chester started a company…: "How can you make and sell your invention…"

2 **2-point response:** In Source #1, the reader is taken through the process of how George Nissen came up with, developed, and named his invention, the trampoline. Using information found in Source #3, the reader can understand the steps he needed to take to patent his invention and keep other people from using his idea. In Source #2, Chester Greenwood patented his improved earmuffs. Source #3 gives the rules for when inventions can be patented, letting the reader know that his ear muffs must have been considered a significant improvement on an old idea.

3 **2-point response:** People invent things because they see that there is a need for something new or because they see a way to make something better. In Source #1, George Nissen thought of a new gymnastics prop. He saw a need for the trampoline that most others could not see, and he spent much of his life helping others see its value. In Source #2, Chester Greenwood needed to find a way to protect his ears from the cold wind. This need led to an improvement in the ear muff important enough to patent.

10-point anchor paper: Have you ever thought you would like to be an inventor? Well, the first step is to come up with an idea for something new. It is also okay to come up with a big improvement on an old idea. Usually, inventions make life easier in some way. The inventions meet a need that people have.

The next step, of course, is to try building the invention if it is something that can be built. It is important to have a clear understanding of how the invention works. This is especially important if you intend to patent it. This is because you will have to show exactly what that would look like and how it will work.

Third, decide how you want to use your invention. If you want everyone to use it for free, then avoid getting a patent. If you want to make a company and earn money, it is probably a good idea to get a patent.

Next, do research to learn what similar things have been invented. This will help you avoid trying to get a patent for something that is already out there. It will also help you learn to describe what makes your invention unique. Finally, apply for the patent. Once your invention is patented, you can create a company that makes your invention available to many.

Answer Key

Name: _____

In Source #1, the reader can see most of this process in the context of Chester Greenwood's invention. He discovered a need, then thought of his invention. He made it with the help of his grandmother, patented it, and formed a company to make and sell his invention.

In Source #2, the reader can see other parts of the process emphasized. For example, George Nissen spent a great deal of energy creating a market for his invention. He needed to help the public see that his idea was a good one in order to be able to sell his invention. Both inventors went through a version of the process that I outline here. Both inventors follow roughly the same process, but it can look very different in different situations. What will you invent, and what will the process look like for you?

Read the text. Then answer the questions.

A Town's History

Lily glanced up at the clock in the front of the classroom. The minute hand was crawling much too slowly. There was still more than an hour until lunchtime and Lily could already hear her stomach complaining. She slumped down in her seat and started to fiddle with the pencils on her desk.

"Is the speaker going to be here soon, Mr. Gardiner?" Kevin eagerly asked the teacher. On Monday, the teacher had told the class that someone would come give a presentation that Friday, but he hadn't told them who it would be. All week, Lily and her classmates had been trying to guess the speaker's identity.

"What about the President?" Steven asked. Everyone laughed at the idea of the President of the United States coming to talk to the fifth-grade glass in their small town in Oregon.

"Okay, class," said Mr. Gardiner. "I will finally tell you the name of our speaker: Ms. Traynor. She works at the local history museum and will be sharing information with us about our town's history."

"History is so boring," Lily thought. "I can't imagine that anything interesting ever happened here."

Just then, there was a knock at the door, and the principal came in with a business-like woman carrying a large briefcase. Mr. Gardiner introduced her to the class.

"Your teacher has told me that you are studying the Oregon Trail," Ms. Traynor said. "Does anyone know how this town is an important part of the trail's history?"

"It's at the very end of the Oregon Trail," Bethany answered. "That's right. Today, I'm going to tell you about some of the first settlers in our town." Ms. Traynor began to pull several old black-and-white photographs from her briefcase,

GO ON →

displaying them for the class. Some were faded at the corners, and most showed people posing stiffly for the camera. Even the children looked serious.

Lily liked looking at the photographs that demonstrated what people had worn back then. One photograph showed a pretty woman standing tall in a long dress with long sleeves and a flowered bonnet. "She must have sweltered in that outfit, like I do when I wear a sweatshirt on a warm day," she thought. The photo made Lily think of what it might have been like to not be able to wear a short-sleeved shirt when she wanted to, or enjoy air-conditioning!

"One of the ways we study history is to read the letters and journals written by the people of the time," Ms. Traynor explained.

"Where do you get the journals and letters?" was Steven's query.

"People donate them to the museum so we don't have to buy them. Many of the people who live here are descendants of the first settlers. Sometimes people have saved letters and journals from their great-grandparents. Other people find old journals and mementos when they are cleaning out their houses. I am going to share some of these historic treasures with you today."

In one letter, a woman wrote to her sister back east describing her journey on the Oregon Trail. She told of long, hot, dusty days on the trail and cold nights camping with the wagons circled around them. She had written about crossing a river on a small, wooden raft that was rocked by the strong rapids. Some of her belongings had fallen into the river, but she had been relieved to make it safely to the other side.

When Ms. Traynor passed around a journal that had been discovered in someone's attic, Lily couldn't wait to look at it. It had been written by a girl around Lily's age. She turned the pages of the small book carefully. She saw that the girl had written about her new town and her new school. The girl had been nervous about beginning school in a place where she didn't know anyone, but the other students had made her feel welcome. She had even met her new best friend at the new school.

Then suddenly, Ms. Traynor said, "I know you all have to go to lunch, so we will end our discussion here."

Lily looked up at the clock and saw that it was already 12:30. The hour had flown by. Then Lily thought about her grandmother's attic. She knew her grandmother kept family letters and journals. What kinds of stories could Lily find in those journals? She couldn't wait to find out.

1 The following question has two parts. First, answer part A. Then, answer part B.

Part A: Read the sentence from the text.

"She must have <u>sweltered</u> in that outfit, like I do when I wear a sweatshirt on a warm day," she thought.

What does <u>sweltered</u> mean as it is used in the sentence?

Ⓐ looked nice

Ⓑ felt overly hot

Ⓒ been proud of herself

Ⓓ thought she was stylish

Part B: Which phrase from the sentence **best** shows how Lily relates to the woman's clothing in the photograph?

Ⓐ "must have"

Ⓑ "in that outfit"

Ⓒ "like I do"

Ⓓ "warm day"

2 Read the sentence from the text.

"Where do you get the journals and letters?" was Steven's <u>query</u>.

The word <u>query</u> comes from the Latin word *quaere*, meaning "ask." What does <u>query</u> mean in the sentence above?

Ⓐ interruption

Ⓑ question

Ⓒ reaction

Ⓓ remark

GO ON →

3 The following question has two parts. First, answer part A. Then, answer part B.

Part A: What is the theme of the text?

(A) History can be interesting.

(B) Some surprises are pleasant.

(C) Traveling on the Oregon Trail was hard.

(D) People should keep journals about what they do.

Part B: Which detail from the text **best** supports your answer in part A?

(A) "All week, Lily and her classmates had been trying to guess the speaker's identity."

(B) "'That's right. Today, I'm going to tell you about some of the first settlers in our town.'"

(C) "'Other people find old journals and mementos when they are cleaning out their houses.'"

(D) "What kinds of stories could Lily find in those journals? She couldn't wait to find out."

4 Read the sentence from the text.

"People donate them to the museum so we don't have to buy them."

How does the phrase "don't have to buy" help you understand the meaning of donate in the sentence?

(A) It tells why people do not like to spend money.

(B) It shows that the speaker works in a museum.

(C) It describes people who are interested in history.

(D) It explains what happens when people give things to museums.

GO ON →

5 How does the use of dialogue help the reader understand Lily's feelings? Select **two** options.

(A) by telling Lily's thoughts

(B) by telling what Lily says

(C) by showing Lily's reactions

(D) by describing what Lily does

(E) by showing how others react to Lily

(F) by describing the expressions on Lily's face

6 Select the details from the text that use sensory language. Not all details will be used.

(A) "her new town and her new school"

(B) "long, hot, dusty days on the trail"

(C) "cold nights camping with the wagons circled around them"

(D) "faded at the corners"

(E) "rocked by the strong rapids"

(F) "letters and journals from their great-grandparents"

GO ON →

7 Explain why Lily's feelings about history change as a result of Ms. Traynor's visit to the class. Support your response with examples from the text.

_____

_____

_____

_____

_____

_____

Read the text. Then answer the questions.

Tiny Wintry World

Hold the glass globe in your hands and turn it over gently. Then flip it back and watch as snow falls slowly over a tiny village. For kids and grownups everywhere, snow globes hold a special delight. Yet these fun keepsakes actually came to be because of an experiment that did not work.

In 1900, a man named Erwin Perzy was trying to figure out a way to create more light. Perzy lived in Vienna, Austria, and he made tools to be used for surgery. At that time, the electric light bulb had just been invented, but it created inadequate light. A surgeon asked Perzy to come up with a way to make the light brighter for his operating room.

Perzy contemplated the problem carefully. He remembered how shoemakers would use a special trick to get more light from candles. They would place a glass globe full of water in front of the flame. The light would shine through the globe and cast a golden glow about the size of a hand.

With this in mind, Perzy filled a glass globe with water and placed it in front of his electric light. He was not satisfied with how bright it was, so he decided to add to the idea. First, he tried adding glitter to the water. When it first dropped into the water, the glitter reflected the light and added brightness to the room. However, it sank to the bottom, and the shining effect was gone.

Although his first idea had failed, Perzy felt he was onto something. He tried to find a material that weighed even less than the glitter. After searching, he came upon a fine white powder called semolina. It was usually used to make baby food. Perzy thought the powder would be perfect for his light globe, so he dropped it in. Once again, the powder made the light brighter, but it also soon came to rest on the bottom of the globe. Perzy's experiment failed again. However, it sparked a new idea. For to Perzy, the sinking white powder looked just like fresh falling snow.

GO ON →

Fascinated by his new discovery, Perzy decided the snow should fall onto something. He took a soft, silvery metal called pewter, which he had in his workshop, and made a tiny model of a famous building in Austria. Perzy placed the little structure into the globe and watched the "snow" fall on it. He became even more excited—surely other people would enjoy his globes as much as he did! Quickly, Perzy got a patent for his "glass globe with snow effect." The patent would prove that he invented it.

Over the next few years, Perzy experimented with different materials to find the right one for his snow. He also tried different miniature buildings. In 1905, Perzy opened a small factory to make the snow globes and they quickly became popular. The Austrian emperor, Franz Josef I, even gave Perzy a special award for his new toy. Soon, snow globes could be found in homes all around the world, from cottages to the White House.

Today, Perzy's company, Original Vienna Snow Globes, still produces hundreds of thousands of snow globes each year. Each one is handmade. There are more than 2,000 scenes to choose from, including buildings, animals, nature scenes, and characters. Perzy's family has continued his work, and Erwin Perzy III now runs the company.

Erwin Perzy III really enjoys seeing children visit the company and its museum. Even though snow globes do not have batteries, bright lights, or fun noises, kids are fascinated with them. ". . . When the kids come here," he says, "their eyes are wide open, they are enchanted, and everyone has one or two snow globes in their hands, and they are shaking them. That is a very nice moment for me." While his grandfather's experiment long ago did not work, it actually led to something even more wonderful.

GO ON →

8 The following question has two parts. First, answer part A. Then, answer part B.

Part A: Read the sentences from the text.

At that time, the electric light bulb had just been invented, but it created inadequate light. A surgeon asked Perzy to come up with a way to make the light brighter for his operating room.

What is **most likely** the meaning of the word inadequate?

(A) unclean

(B) expensive

(C) difficult to find

(D) not enough

Part B: Which phrase from the sentences **best** supports your answer in part A?

(A) "electric light bulb"

(B) "just been invented"

(C) "make the light brighter"

(C) "for his operating room"

9 Which statement **best** represents the author's point of view about Perzy?

(A) Perzy was not skilled in using electricity.

(B) Perzy was not creative enough to be an inventor.

(C) Perzy was able to learn from his failures.

(D) Perzy was mainly interested in surgical tools.

GO ON →

10 The following question has two parts. First, answer part A. Then, answer part B.

Part A: Read the sentences from the text.

Perzy contemplated the problem carefully. He remembered how shoemakers would use a special trick to get more light from candles.

What does contemplated mean in the sentence above?

(A) changed around

(B) solved quickly

(C) thought about

(D) worried over

Part B: Which word from the sentences helps you understand the meaning of contemplated?

(A) carefully

(B) remembered

(C) special

(D) candles

11 Read the sentences from the text.

He took a soft, silvery metal called pewter, which he had in his workshop, and made a tiny model of a famous building in Austria. Perzy placed the little structure into the globe and watched the "snow" fall on it.

Which words from the sentences help to define structure? Select **all** that apply.

(A) metal

(B) pewter

(C) workshop

(D) model

(E) building

(F) snow

GO ON →

12 Complete the sentences about the main idea of the text. Circle **one** main idea and **one** detail.

The main idea in "Tiny Wintry World" is that _____. This is **best** supported by the detail, _____.

Main Idea	Detail
snow globes made Erwin Perzy famous	"because of an experiment that did not work"
snow globes were discovered accidentally	"even gave Perzy a special award for his new toy"
snow globes can have different kinds of scenes inside	"including buildings, animals, nature scenes, and characters"

GO ON →

13 Why did the author **most likely** choose to write about Erwin Perzy? Support your answer with details from the text.

_____

_____

_____

_____

_____

_____

14 Select **three** details that **best** support the main idea of the text.

(A) Erwin Perzy's first invention failed.

(B) Erwin Perzy III now runs the snow globe company.

(C) Erwin Perzy used semolina in his first snow globe.

(D) Erwin Perzy originally made tools used for surgery.

(E) Erwin Perzy's company makes its snow globes by hand.

(F) Erwin Perzy thought the falling while powder looked like fresh snow.

GO ON →

Read the texts. Then answer the questions.

Finding Gold, Finding Florida

In 1493, Christopher Columbus sailed again to the Americas. He and others surmised that he had found islands near Asia on his first trip, and for that reason, the crew on this trip numbered 1,500 men on 17 ships. One of the crewmen was Juan Ponce de León. He stayed in the New World after Columbus returned to Spain.

Ponce de León was a skilled soldier. He helped defend the Spanish settlers on the island of Hispaniola from native attacks. As a reward, he was named a governor of the island.

The natives told stories and legends of the area, and one told of an island to the east called Borinquen where there was gold. Ponce de León was sent to explore the island. When the Spanish landed, they had to fight the native Taíno people. The Spanish won, partly because they used dogs in battle. The natives had never seen dogs before, and these fearsome animals were more frightening than the soldiers.

Ponce de León built the first European settlement on Borinquen in 1508. The Spanish soon found gold and forced the native people to mine it. The island was renamed Puerto Rico, meaning "rich port." Ponce de León quickly became rich.

The king then allowed Ponce de León to claim areas north of Hispaniola for Spain, but the king did not provide any ships. Ponce de León used his own wealth to buy ships and supplies. Natives told of an island called Bimini to the north where he could find more gold.

They may have also mentioned a spring that could make people young again. Today, Ponce de León is best known for searching for this "fountain of youth." But there is no proof that Ponce de León ever heard the legend, since none of his writings survived. He did believe he was close to Asia, and he may have known that Alexander the Great of Macedonia had unsuccessfully searched for a fountain of youth in Asia 1,800 years before. If Ponce de León did search for a similar source of youth, his search was as fruitless as Alexander the Great's.

GO ON →

The ships sailed north in 1513. They made a few stops at islands in the Bahamas. When they saw the coast of Florida, they thought it was an island, too. They probably landed first near modern-day St. Augustine. They claimed the land for Spain. Ponce de León named it La Florida, meaning "the place of flowers." He must have noted the rainbow colors and sweet smells of the flowers.

His ships sailed down the east coast of Florida. They stopped on islands they named the Dry Tortugas, where they found little fresh water but many large sea turtles. Sea turtles are called *tortugas* in Spanish. Later, they tried to land on the west coast of Florida. They soon found that the Calusa people living there were not friendly, so they left Florida and returned to Puerto Rico.

In 1521, Ponce de León returned to the west coast of Florida. He had two ships and 200 men. They wanted to build a settlement, but the Calusa people attacked them again. Ponce de León was wounded in the leg with an arrow. Some thought it was poisoned. The Spanish returned to Puerto Rico, where Ponce de León died soon afterward.

Other explorers realized before long that Florida was not an island and was not in Asia. Spain controlled many areas in the Caribbean and Latin America for more than 300 years. Ponce de León did not find a fountain of youth, but his voyages spurred others to search for gold and other riches in the New World.

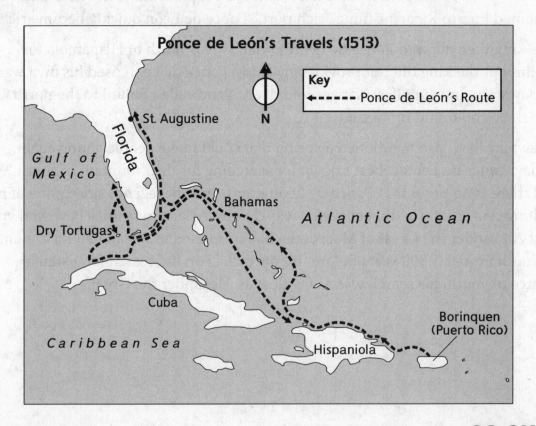

Ponce de León's Travels (1513)

Key
◄------- Ponce de León's Route

GO ON →

Pioneering in Florida

Ben Hill Doster moved his family from Atlanta, Georgia, to Jupiter, Florida, in 1894 to help his sister. Her husband had died, but she hoped to own 160 acres of land there as a homestead. She just needed to live on it for one more year.

Soon after they arrived, Ben Doster took his family on a boat ride up the Loxahatchee River. Suddenly, the air turned cold. Feeling agitated, Doster rowed hurriedly back to the tiny cabin, and the family huddled inside near a roaring fire. That night they heard sounds like gunshots, but the sounds turned out to be the trunks of orange trees exploding when they froze. The next morning, they awoke to find their 16-acre pineapple patch frozen and their garden vegetables dead.

Many new settlers left soon after the Big Freeze of 1894, but the Doster family stayed. They replanted their pineapples and their garden, and they also opened up a general store. Slowly, Doster's wife and two daughters learned to love the land of southern Florida and respect its dangers.

In their first year, they began to recognize the sounds of the swamp at night. They thought of it as a nightly serenade; different types of frogs had distinctive calls. The tiniest frogs chirped "tea table, tea table." The bullfrogs boomed "rung, rung, rung." Owls hooted and birds called to their mates. Sometimes, alligators bellowed.

But one night they awoke to hear the painful scream of a woman. She sounded like she was nearby, so Mrs. Doster prepared to go outside to look for her. But Ben Doster stopped her at the door. He explained that when panthers screamed in the night, they sounded exactly like a woman in pain. No one should go outside to help, because panthers were dangerous.

GO ON →

The family gradually came to know their neighbors and the people who came to the Dosters' store. Some were homesteaders like themselves and included the local doctor and a man who had gone to Princeton University in New Jersey. Another neighbor claimed to be a member of an English royal family.

Other people had been in the area for generations. These included a few African Americans, descendants of enslaved people who had fled to Florida in the early 1800s. Other families were descendants of early white settlers. They lived in the swamps and continued to make their living by hunting, trapping, and fishing. Sometimes families of Seminole Indians would suddenly appear, using trails through the swamps that no one else could follow. They would camp near a trail to sell deer and alligator hides, bird feathers, and dried venison from deer hunting. They were members of the few families who survived the Seminole Wars of the 1800s and the removal of most of the Seminoles to reservations in the West.

One of Doster's daughters, Dora, later wrote about her memories of the time. She wrote lovingly of mangrove and cypress trees hung with Spanish moss. She saw white herons standing like statues waiting to pluck fish from the shallow water. Yellow and orange butterflies danced down a path in front of her. She thought the ocean before a hurricane looked like a vicious monster, curling its jaws and showing its teeth. She learned to watch for the poisonous snakes that lived along the paths.

Dora's mother was a strong and brave woman. She stood up to panthers, alligators, and hurricanes. But for her, there was more than danger, beauty, and excitement. Dora's father worked long hours at the store. Dora thought her mother must have gotten very homesick and lonely at the cabin. She saw her mother watch the trains pass to the east and listen to their mournful wails. Dora believed she often wanted to be on one of those trains, headed back home. She had grown up in Atlanta and had not planned to become a pioneer.

GO ON →

Answer these questions about "Finding Gold, Finding Florida."

15 Read the sentence from the text.

The natives had never seen dogs before, and these <u>fearsome</u> animals were more frightening than the soldiers.

What does the word <u>fearsome</u> mean in the sentence above?

(A) strong

(B) strange

(C) terrifying

(D) interesting

16 Explain how the map contributes to a clearer understanding of the text. Use **two** details from the article to support your answer.

_____

_____

_____

_____

_____

_____

GO ON →

17 Match **one** key detail with **each** main idea from the text.

Ponce de León was a gifted soldier.

| With the help of dogs, he defeated the Taíno people. |

| Instead of using the king's money, he used his own to buy ships. |

Ponce de León was a loyal explorer.

| He paved the way for future voyagers who were spurred by his adventures. |

| As a reward for helping Spanish settlers, he became a governor. |

GO ON →

Answer these questions about "Pioneering in Florida."

18 The following question has two parts. First, answer part A. Then, answer part B.

Part A: Why did the Doster family move to Florida?

(A) Ben Doster's wife wanted to have new experiences.

(B) Ben Doster wanted to help his sister get her homestead.

(C) The Doster family wanted to become fruit growers.

(D) The Dosters wanted their children to grow up away from the city.

Part B: Which phrase from the text supports your answer in part A?

(A) "needed to live on it for one more year"

(B) "took his family on a boat ride"

(C) "they heard sounds like gunshots"

(D) "replanted their pineapples and their garden"

19 Read the sentence from the text.

"Yellow and orange butterflies danced down a path in front of her."

What does the use of the phrase "danced down a path" suggest about the butterflies?

(A) They were moving in pairs.

(B) They were blocking a walkway.

(C) They were responding to music.

(D) They were lively and graceful.

GO ON →

20 What can you conclude about the author's attitude toward the Dosters and how they adjusted to life in Florida? Use **two** details from the text to support your conclusion.

_____

_____

_____

_____

_____

Name: _____ Date: _____

Answer these questions about "Finding Gold, Finding Florida" and "Pioneering in Florida."

21 Explain how the Dosters and Ponce de León were both exploring a "new world." Use details from **both** texts to describe their different experiences.

_____
_____
_____
_____
_____
_____
_____
_____
_____
_____
_____
_____

GO ON →

The text below needs revision. Read the text. Then answer the questions.

(1) Penicillin, one of our most important drugs, come from mold. (2) Alexander Fleming discovered it in England—by accident!

(3) In 1922, Fleming was trying to figure out how to kill bacteria that caused diseases. (4) He has a cold and his nose is runny. (5) When he picked up a lab dish, some mucus from his nose dripped into it. (6) He seen that the mucus killed the bacteria growing in the dish. (7) By accident, he had made an important discovery. (8) It made him want to keep searching.

(9) In 1928, Fleming piled some lab dishes in a tray of liquid chemicals. (10) The chemicals would sterilize them. (11) But some of the dishes didn't get covered by the chemicals. (12) Later, he noticed that mold had growed on one of the dishes. (13) The mold had killed the bacteria!

(14) The importance of Fleming's discovery wasn't realized right away. (15) It wasn't until about 1940 that penicillin became widely used in medicine. (16) Since then, penicillin has cured some diseases that once killed millions of people.

(17) Fleming was very lucky. (18) But he wouldn't have succeeded if he hadn't been working hard on experiments anyway. (19) His discoveries was a combination of luck and hard work.

GO ON →

22 How can sentence 1 **best** be written?

(A) One of our most important drugs, penicillin come from mold.

(B) One of our most important drugs, mold, comes from penicillin.

(C) Penicillin, one of our most important drugs, comes from mold.

(D) Penicillin, one of our most important drugs, coming from mold.

23 Which sentence has an action verb?

(A) Sentence 2

(B) Sentence 4

(C) Sentence 17

(D) Sentence 19

24 Which sentence incorrectly shifts tense from past to present?

(A) Sentence 2

(B) Sentence 3

(C) Sentence 4

(D) Sentence 5

25 How can sentence 6 **best** be written?

(A) He see that the mucus killed the bacteria growing in the dish.

(B) He saw that the mucus killed the bacteria growing in the dish.

(C) He seen that the mucus killed the bacteria growing in the dish.

(D) He was seeing that the mucus killed the bacteria growing in the dish.

GO ON →

26 What is the **best** way to write sentence 12?

(A) Later, he noticed that mold was grown on one of the dishes.

(B) Later, he noticed that mold growed on one of the dishes.

(C) Later, he noticed that mold grow on one of the dishes.

(D) Later, he noticed that mold had grown on one of the dishes.

27 Which sentence uses the past progressive tense?

(A) Sentence 2

(B) Sentence 3

(C) Sentence 5

(D) Sentence 7

28 Which sentence indicates that Fleming's work was on-going?

(A) Sentence 8

(B) Sentence 9

(C) Sentence 17

(D) Sentence 18

29 Which sentence uses a helping verb with a main verb?

(A) Sentence 6

(B) Sentence 9

(C) Sentence 10

(D) Sentence 19

GO ON →

30 Which sentence uses a linking verb?

- **A** Sentence 1
- **B** Sentence 6
- **C** Sentence 11
- **D** Sentence 17

31 Which sentence has an error in subject-verb agreement?

- **A** Sentence 16
- **B** Sentence 17
- **C** Sentence 18
- **D** Sentence 19

STOP

Opinion Performance Task

Task:

Your class has been learning about bees and their positive and negative aspects. Now your school board has announced that it is considering allowing a local company to donate materials, and train the students and staff to raise bees at the school. Your principal has asked students to write a multi-paragraph essay that explains your opinion about the plan to the school board. Before you begin, you do some research and find two articles, and a video about bees and beekeeping.

After you have reviewed these sources, you will answer some questions about them. Briefly scan the sources and the three questions that follow. Then go back and review the sources carefully to gain the information you will need to answer the questions and finalize your research. You may take notes on the information you find in the sources as you read. Your notes will be available to you as you answer the questions.

Directions for Part 1

You will now examine several sources. You can reexamine any of the sources as often as you like.

Research Questions:

After examining the sources, use the remaining time in Part I to answer the three questions. Your answers to these questions will be scored. Also, your answers will help you think about the sources you have read, and viewed, which should help you write your opinion essay.

You may look at your notes when you think it would be helpful.

GO ON →

Source #1: A Golden Treasure

In ancient Greece, one wise man thought honey trickled down into the sky from rainbows, and bees gathered the drops from the air. Today, people know bees make honey in their hives. The busy insects must collect nectar from two million flowers to produce one pound of honey. Their hard work gives us a special food.

A Tasty Treasure

For thousands of years, people have valued honey for its sweet flavors. Sometimes, these flavors vary. The taste of the honey depends on the nectar the bees collect. For instance, if the busy bees gather nectar mainly from orange blossoms, the honey is pale yellow and mild. In contrast, honey produced from buckwheat flowers is very dark and strong-tasting.

People have prized honey because it is an easy food to store, too. In fact, scientists digging in Egypt found some honey in a jar in a tomb. The golden food was still fine to eat.

Honey seldom spoils because it consists of little water. As a result, germs cannot easily grow in the syrupy liquid. Sometimes, the lack of water causes the honey to form crystals and turn into a gooey lump. When this happens, the honey remains safe to eat. Warming the jar in some hot water solves the problem.

Super Powers

While people simply enjoy honey's sweet taste, scientists have discovered the food offers other key benefits. One study tested honey samples from various regions in the country. In this way, different kinds of honey, such as clover honey or alfalfa honey, were included. Scientists found that all the honey samples contained certain vitamins and minerals. These vitamins and minerals are an important part of a healthy diet.

Honey also contains a sugar called glucose. Studies show that glucose from honey helps a person's stomach digest and absorb foods. For instance, eating honey increased the amount of calcium a person absorbed by 25%. The body can use this extra calcium for building bones.

GO ON →

Soothing and Healing

Honey has other surprising uses. When a person has a cold, honey works as well as a medicine to stop the cough. In one study, scientists examined 270 children who had ordinary coughs. Some of them took two teaspoonfuls of honey before they went to sleep for the night. Others swallowed a few spoonfuls of sweetened water. The children who ate the honey coughed less and slept more soundly.

In addition, some people use honey to heal minor scrapes. The thick liquid seals the wound and kills germs. The vitamins in honey help the body grow new blood vessels and skin. However, a doctor should always care for serious wounds.

Today, scientists continue to study honey. They are testing whether it can kill germs that cause food poisoning. They are investigating whether it can help people with allergies. Every day, this amazing food grows more valuable. Thank you, bees!

GO ON →

Source #2: Beekeeping for Beginners

A strange squat tower hides behind some bushes in a backyard. Before long, some honeybees disappear inside the structure; it is a hive box for bees. Today, there are beekeepers in every state in America. With the right supplies and some preparation, you can try this popular hobby, too.

Beehive Basics

First, you will need a home for your bees. Usually, beginners purchase a modern hive box. It contains different sections, and each one serves a specific purpose.

The base of the box includes the hive stand and bottom board. The hive stand has a slanted front edge that resembles a small slide. Bees loaded with pollen can safely land on the inclined board and creep inside their home.

The top of the hive has both outer and inner covers. The outer cover acts like a lid, neatly fitting over the hive's edges. It protects the hive from stormy weather and gusty winds. The inner cover is a flat board. This barrier prevents bees from attaching their sticky honey to the lid.

In the center of the hive, there are several crate-shaped boxes, or "supers." The bottom super is the brood chamber, where the queen bee lays her eggs. Eventually, they hatch into larvae, which resemble white, curved worms. Next, the larvae grow into pupae, with bodies shaped like bees. Finally, they become adults.

Directly above the brood chamber is the honey super. In this location, the bees construct their honeycomb and fill its waxy cells with honey. Every hive contains one honey super, but you can easily add more.

Special Equipment

Beekeeping does not require many tools, but a few are necessary. One essential object is a smoker. This machine releases little clouds of smoke when pumped. The smoke does not harm the bees, but it causes them to start consuming honey. After their meal, the bees are sleepy, so they are simpler to manage.

You will also need a bee veil, hat, and gloves. These clothing items guard against stings. In addition, some people wear bee suits, but a light-colored shirt and pants work well, too. Most importantly, clothing should always be clean and odor-free. Bees have a remarkable sense of smell, and numerous scents alarm them. If the bees are frightened, they may sting.

GO ON →

Ready for Bees

Most first-time beekeepers order bees for their hive from an established, trusted company. A box will arrive in the mail containing about 10,000 worker bees and one queen. To add them to your hive, you can consult a beekeeping guide and follow its instructions.

Caring for Your Hive

Typically, the bees quickly adjust to their new home and begin their tasks. The queen spends her time laying eggs in the brood chamber, while the workers forage for flowers full of pollen. The bees devote themselves to building a honey supply and strengthening their numbers.

In the summer, you should regularly check on your growing hive. You can add more honey supers if needed and occasionally remove some honey. At times, you should inspect the brood chamber to make sure the queen and the young bees are healthy.

In the winter, your hive needs little maintenance; the bees remain secure inside. However, you must be sure to leave enough honey to sustain the colony during the cold months.

Do you think you would like to try beekeeping? To gather more helpful information, visit a local beekeeper. Most beekeepers are excited to share their experiences and love for their hobby with newcomers.

Source #3: Controlling Problem Honeybees

Honeybees are valuable insects. They produce honey, and they help plants grow by spreading pollen. However, bees near homes can become a nuisance. To control these problem bees, you must understand their behavior and habits. The following information will provide some useful tips to guide you.

Keep Things Clean

Normally, honeybees rely on pollen as their main source of food, but they will eat other available fare. Sweet treats such as juices, sugar, and fruits attract them. In the late summer, when fewer flowers bloom, bees especially seek these easy meals.

Because of this, outside dining areas and open trash cans appeal to bees. The key to discouraging the bees is cleanliness. Always line trash cans with bags and shut their lids. After eating outdoors, wash off patio tables and wipe up spills. Close food bags and bring leftover snacks inside.

Recycling bins filled with dirty cans and bottles draw bees, too. You should cover the bins with some type of barrier. If necessary, use an old door screen or window. While the job takes time, it is important to stop the first bees from entering the bins. These bees will share their find with other hive members, and large numbers will soon arrive.

Watch and Wait

In the late spring, you may spy a big swarm of bees on a tree near your home. This happens when a crowded bee colony sends off some bees to start a new hive. The buzzing mass clusters in a temporary resting place such as a branch.

While the swarm looks threatening, these insects are not aggressive. The bees have no hive to defend, so they are not likely to sting. Once their scouts find a suitable location to build their next home, the bees will leave. If possible, the best approach is to be patient for a few days and wait for them to go.

GO ON →

Time for Experts

Unfortunately, sometimes scouting bees select the wall of a building for their new home. They find a way inside through a tiny crack or hole. Slowly, the bees begin to build a hive in the space.

When you notice bees entering a crack on the outside of your house, it is tempting to spray their doorway with bug spray. However, this plan is not wise for several reasons. First, the bee hive may be far inside the wall, and the spray will not reach it. Also, the spray could cause the bees to look for another exit and encourage them to enter your home. Finally, the spray may kill some bees, but their honey will remain in the wall. The sweet food will attract other insect pests.

Instead, you should call a pest control company. They have the proper tools and supplies to deal with defensive bees. Plus, they will remove the contents of the hive.

Once the experts finish their work, make your own repairs. Patch any cracks and plug entrance holes. Wash the area with soap and apply fresh paint. This will get rid of odors, which could attract future bees.

Today, in our country, honeybees help pollinate about 100 food crops. Most often, they are content to search for pollen and will not bother you. With a little understanding, it is easy to live in peace with these beneficial insects.

GO ON →

Name: _____ Date: _____

1 Source #1 discusses the different behaviors of bees. What do Source #2 and Source #3 explain about bee behavior that Source #1 does not? Draw a line from the source to the description of bee behavior. Not all descriptions will be used.

Source #2: Beekeeping for Beginners   Honey is beneficial to humans in many ways.

Source #3: Controlling Problem Honeybees   Bees send out scouts to look for a new place to build a hive.

                                                       The practice of beekeeping is in every state in America.

2 What positive aspects of bees are presented in the sources? Provide specific details from at least **two** sources in your answer. For each example, include the source title or number.

_____

_____

_____

_____

_____

GO ON →

3 Explain why it is important to protect bees. Give **two** reasons why bees are
valuable, **one** from Source #1 and **one** from Source #3. For each reason, include
the source title and number.

_____

_____

_____

_____

_____

_____

_____

GO ON →

Directions for Part 2:

You will now review your notes and sources, and plan, draft, revise, and edit your opinion essay. You may use your notes and refer to the sources. Now read your assignment and the information about how your essay will be scored; then begin your work.

Your Assignment:

Your school board is considering allowing a company to donate "beekeeper kits," and train the students and staff to raise bees at the school. Your principal has asked students to write a multi-paragraph essay to give an opinion about the idea. The audience for your essay will be the principal and the school board. In your essay, clearly state your opinion and support your opinion with reasons that are thoroughly developed using information from what you have read.

Now you are going to write your opinion essay to submit to the principal. Your essay should include information supporting your opinion about beekeeping at your school. Choose the most important information from all three sources to support your ideas. Then, write an opinion essay that is several paragraphs long. Clearly organize your essay and support your ideas with details from the sources. Use your own words except when quoting directly from the sources. Be sure to give the source title or number when using details from the sources.

REMEMBER: A well-written opinion essay

- has a clear opinion
- is well-organized and stays on the topic
- has an introduction and a conclusion
- uses transitions
- uses details from the sources to support your opinion
- develops ideas clearly
- uses clear language
- follows rules of writing (spelling, punctuation, and grammar)

Now begin work on your opinion essay. Manage your time carefully so that you can plan, write, revise, and edit the final draft of your opinion essay. Write your response on a separate sheet of paper.

Answer Key

Name: _____

Question	Correct Answer	Content Focus	CCSS	Complexity
1A	B	Context Clues: Comparison	L.5.4a	DOK 2
1B	C	Context Clues: Comparison/ Text Evidence	L.5.4a/ RL.5.1	DOK 2
2	B	Latin Roots	L.5.4b	DOK 2
3A	A	Theme	RL.5.2	DOK 2
3B	D	Theme/Text Evidence	RL.5.2/ RL.5.1	DOK 2
4	D	Context Clues: Cause and Effect	L.5.4a	DOK 2
5	A, C	Theme	RL.5.2	DOK 3
6	B, C, E	Literary Element: Sensory Language	RL.5.4	DOK 3
7	see below	Theme	RL.5.2	DOK 3
8A	D	Context Clues: Sentence Clues	L.5.4a	DOK 2
8B	C	Context Clues: Sentence Clues/ Text Evidence	L.5.4a/ RI.5.1	DOK 3
9	C	Author's Point of View	RI.5.8	DOK 2
10A	C	Context Clues: Sentence Clues	L.5.4a	DOK 2
10B	B	Context Clues: Sentence Clues/ Text Evidence	L.5.4a/ RI.5.1	DOK 2
11	D, E	Context Clues: Sentence Clues	L.5.4a	DOK 2
12	see below	Main Idea and Key Details	RI.5.2	DOK 3
13	see below	Author's Point of View	RI.5.8	DOK 3
14	A, D, F	Main Idea and Key Details	RI.5.2	DOK 3
15	C	Context Clues: Sentence Clues	L.5.4a	DOK 2
16	see below	Text Features: Diagrams	RI.4.7	DOK 3
17	see below	Main Idea and Key Details.	RI.5.2	DOK 3
18A	B	Main Idea and Key Details	RI.5.2	DOK 2
18B	A	Main Idea and Key Details/ Text Evidence	RI.5.2/ RI.5.1	DOK 3
19	D	Personification	L.5.5a	DOK 2
20	see below	Author's Point of View	RI.5.8	DOK 3
21	see below	Compare Across Texts	RI.5.9	DOK 4

Question	Correct Answer	Content Focus	CCSS	Complexity
22	C	Subject-Verb Agreement	L.3.1f	DOK 1
23	A	Action Verbs	L.3.1a	DOK 1
24	C	Verb Tenses	L.5.1d	DOK 1
25	B	Irregular Verbs	L.3.1d	DOK 1
26	D	Irregular Verbs	L.3.1d	DOK 1
27	B	Verb Tenses	L.4.1b	DOK 1
28	A	Verb Tenses	L.5.1b	DOK 1
29	C	Main Verbs and Helping Verbs	L.5.1	DOK 1
30	D	Linking Verbs	L.5.1	DOK 1
31	D	Subject-Verb Agreement	L.3.1f	DOK 1

Comprehension: Selected Responses 3A, 3B, 5, 6, 9, 12, 14, 17, 18A, 18B	/16	%
Comprehension: Constructed Response 7, 13, 16, 20, 21	/12	%
Vocabulary 1A, 1B, 2, 4, 8A, 8B, 10A, 10B, 11, 15, 19	/16	%
English Language Conventions 22–31	/10	%
Total Unit Assessment Score	/54	%

7 **2-point response:** Ms. Traynor uses local artifacts such as photos, letters, and journals to help the students relate to the people who moved to the town many years ago. By making these kinds of personal connections, Lily begins to see similarities between her own life and the lives people led many years ago.

12 Students should circle the following:
- **Main Idea:** snow globes were discovered accidentally
- **Detail:** "because of an experiment that did not work"

13 **2-point response:** The author sees Erwin Perzy as someone admirable. When a discovery sparked a new idea, Perzy worked on that idea until completion. For example, he encountered several different setbacks with glitter and powder falling to the bottom of his glass globe. He persevered, though, and when he solved his problem he patented the snow globe. Eventually he formed a large company that is still in existence today.

16 **2-point response:** The map provides a diagram of the route of Ponce de León's voyage in 1513. It shows that he started in Puerto Rico, went north to the Bahamas, and then continued north to Florida, where he traveled along both coasts. He then went to Cuba and returned to Puerto Rico. It also shows that he made many stops along his way.

Name: _____

17 Students should match the following:
- Gifted soldier: With the help of dogs, he defeated the Taíno people.
- Loyal explorer: Instead of using the king's money, he used his own to buy ships.

20 **2-point response:** The author believes the Dosters adjusted bravely to the difficulties they faced in Florida. The Big Freeze of 1894 destroyed their orange trees, pineapples, and vegetables. Even though many other families left Florida because of the freeze, the Dosters did not. The author also states that Dora's mother "stood up to panthers, alligators, and hurricanes" and that the Dosters slowly "learned to love the land of Southern Florida and respect its dangers."

21 **4-point response:** Ponce de León went to the New World to discover and claim new lands, while the Dosters went to Florida to help a family member. Florida was a dangerous place for both the Dosters and Ponce de León. Ponce de León was the first European to explore, claim, and settle lands such as Puerto Rico and Florida. He found gold and became rich from it, but he was unable to establish a settlement in Florida or to find a fountain of youth (if he was searching for it). The Dosters experienced the beauty and dangers of a new area in the wilderness of Florida. They helped Ben Doster's sister keep her land and in the process made a new family home.

Opinion Performance Task				
Question	**Answer**	**CCSS**	**Complexity**	**Score**
1	see below	RI.5.1, RI.5.2, RI.5.7, RI.5.8, RI.5.9 W.5.1a-d, W.5.3, W.5.4, W.5.7 L.5.1, L.5.2	DOK 2	/1
2	see below		DOK 3	/2
3	see below		DOK 3	/2
Opinion Essay	see below		DOK 4	/4 [P/O] /4 [E/E] /2 [C]
Total Score				**/15**

1 Students should match the following:
- Source #2: The practice of beekeeping is in every state in America.
- Source #3: Bees send out scouts to look for a place to build a new hive.

2 **2-point response:** Source #1 explains the health benefits of honey. These include aiding digestion, increasing calcium absorption, calming coughs, and healing scrapes. Source # 2 explains the ease and popularity of caring for honeybees. Source #3 explains that honeybees produce valuable honey and help plants grow through pollination.

3 **2-point response:** Bees are valuable to people for many reasons. Source #1 explains a number of reasons why the honey produced by honeybees is beneficial. For example, scientists are studying honey and its ability to kill germs and assist people with allergies. Source #3 explains that bees are valuable because they are responsible for spreading the pollen that helps plants grow. Today honeybees help pollinate about 100 food crops in the United States.

10-point anchor paper: Last year, I walked too close to a beehive and the bees in the hive swarmed down on me. I was stung several times. Ever since that time, I have been terrified of bees. If this company's plan to make beekeepers of my classmates becomes real, I will have a problem. I will have to learn to swallow my fear, and everyone else like me will have to do the same. I want to help stop this idea before it goes any further.

I realize that bees make honey, the "golden treasure," as the author of Source #1 calls it, and I like honey. I also realize that honey has many important health benefits. For one thing, honey seems to protect people from allergies. "Honeybees are valuable insects," the author of Source #3 writes, but the same author also writes, "bees near homes can become a nuisance."

The problem is that putting a beehive in our school can create a problem for everyone in the school. After flowers stop blooming in the late summer, the bees look for other kinds of food than nectar and pollen. The author of Source #3 states that sweet "treats such as juices, sugar, and fruits attract" bees. This means that if the bees cannot find what they need, they could fly all around the school looking for food in garbage containers and even in leftover cans and bottles.

Late spring is another problem season. Bees from one nest will leave to look for a place to build a new nest. According to Source #3, they will sometimes look for cracks in the walls of buildings to build a nest. I do not blame the bees for this, but I don't want them nesting all over the school.

As the author of Source #2 shows that beekeeping can be an interesting hobby. People get to watch all the life stages of bees. I would try it myself if bees did not sting. Unfortunately, bees do sting, and they terrify some people, like me. Before the school board decides to invite thousands of new bees into our school, it should think hard about how this decision will affect everyone in the school.

Read the text. Then answer the questions.

Learning from Folk Medicine

Today, when we are sick, we can go to a doctor for treatment. Doctors have found cures and treatments for many diseases. Modern medicine has been extremely valuable to humanity. It has helped people survive serious diseases and suffer less pain.

Before modern medicine, people also had ways to help those who were sick. They turned to nature to find cures. They discovered plants that could be used to heal or treat illnesses. When they found something that worked, they would share the remedy with others. This information was passed down from one generation to another. It is often called folk medicine.

Many people think that we can't learn anything from folk medicine. But that is not true. You might be surprised to find out how many modern medicines are based on old folk remedies.

Many folk remedies used tree bark as an ingredient. The native peoples of Canada and the United States used the bark of the chokecherry tree to treat colds and coughs. After they removed the bark from the tree, they would dry it, then boil the proper amount and make a tea. The tea tasted good and made people feel better. Modern scientists discovered that the tea does soothe people's sore throats. It also allows the person to heal more swiftly because of the nutrients it contains. Nowadays the bark is used as a flavoring in some cough syrups.

GO ON →

Malaria is a deadly disease in some countries. Long ago, the Inca of South America found a way to treat malaria. They made a medicine using the bark of the cinchona tree. In the 1600s, Spanish explorers were surprised to see the Incan people using cinchona powder to treat malaria effectively. Later, the Spanish sent the powder to other regions where the disease was also a problem. People in other areas also successfully used the powder. Cinchona powder was used for over 200 years before a scientist studied it. He realized that a specific chemical in the tree bark helped fight the disease. The chemical was named quinine after the Incan word for "tree bark." Quinine is still used today to treat malaria.

The Incan people used cinchona powder, which contains quinine, to treat malaria.

The Japanese have known for hundreds of years that eating a type of red seaweed would help them with intestinal problems. Not long ago, scientists discovered that this red seaweed contains kainic acid, which can be used in medicine. The medicine is used to get rid of parasites in the intestines.

GO ON →

For centuries, traditional healers in the British Isles used a flowering plant called foxglove to treat ulcers, bruises, and other problems. One of its main uses was for edema, or the buildup of fluid in the body. An 18th-century English doctor showed that this problem was often associated with heart failure and that foxglove had a positive effect on the heart muscle. (However, it is highly poisonous in the wrong doses.) Today, a drug called digitalis is made from foxglove leaves. The drug is prescribed for people with certain heart problems.

Plant	Used in Folk Medicine	Modern Use
chokecherry bark	colds and coughs	Bark is used to make cough syrup flavoring.
cinchona bark	malaria	Quinine (chemical in bark) is used to treat malaria.
red seaweed	intestinal problems	Kainic acid (in red seaweed) kills intestinal parasites.
foxglove leaves	edema	Digitalis (made from the leaves) affects the heart muscle and helps with certain heart disease.

People are often quick to reject or ignore ideas from the past. They don't think we can learn anything from folk medicine. But as these examples show, we shouldn't ignore old ideas. Scientists can base new medicines on old remedies. Scientists are still researching some of the plants and other ingredients used in folk medicine. Who knows what old remedy will become a new medicine?

GO ON →

Name: _____ **Date:** _____

1 Draw a line from **each** word in column A to the word in column B that has almost the same meaning.

Column A	Column B
disease	treatment
cure	illness
modern	current
	traditional
	nature
	information

2 Read the sentence from the text.

Modern medicine has been extremely valuable to humanity.

How does the author support this statement? Select **two** options.

(A) "Cinchona powder was used for over 200 years before a scientist studied it."

(B) "Nowadays the bark is used as a flavoring in some cough syrups."

(C) "Doctors have found cures and treatments for many diseases."

(D) "Many people think that we can't learn anything from folk medicine."

(E) "It has helped people survive serious diseases and suffer less pain."

(F) "Today, a drug called digitalis is made from foxglove leaves."

GO ON →

122

Grade 5 • Unit Assessment • Unit 4

Copyright © McGraw-Hill Education.

3 The following question has two parts. First, answer part A. Then, answer part B.

Part A: Read the sentences from the text.

They discovered plants that could be used to heal or treat illnesses. When they found something that worked, they would share the <u>remedy</u> with others.

What does the word <u>remedy</u> mean?

Ⓐ a solution

Ⓑ an experiment

Ⓒ an interesting type of news

Ⓓ a secret piece of information

Part B: Which phrase from the sentences supports your answer in part A?

Ⓐ "discovered plants"

Ⓑ "to heal or treat"

Ⓒ "found something"

Ⓓ "with others"

GO ON →

4 What is the purpose of the illustration in the text? Select **two** options.

(A) to suggest Incan healers had good educations

(B) to provide an example of a risky folk medicine

(C) to explain difficulties of the Incan way of life

(D) to show that modern medicine comes from old practices

(E) to demonstrate how the Spanish learned about cinchona

(F) to help the reader understand the author's viewpoint

5 Read the sentence from the text.

People are often quick to reject or ignore ideas from the past.

Which word is an antonym of reject?

(A) accept

(B) deny

(C) praise

(D) imitate

GO ON →

6 Which title **best** describes the chart in the text?

(A) How Folk Medicine and Modern Medicine Are Different

(B) Examples of Folk Medicines with Modern Uses

(C) Substances for Making Tea

(D) Trees Doctors Can Use

7 Explain why the author believes that folk medicine and modern medicine have much in common. Use **two** details from the text to support your answer.

_____

_____

_____

_____

_____

_____

GO ON →

Read the text. Then answer the questions.

A Day with Grandpa

As soon as I asked, I knew the answer. All I wanted to do was go with my friend Ethan to watch the new *Space Dangers* movie. Unfortunately, my mom had other plans.

"You need to spend some time with your grandfather, Josh. You see Ethan every day." Mom answered.

"But, Mom," I whined, "he never wants to do anything interesting." I knew that my grandfather was visiting for only a short time, but the things he wanted to do were always boring. However, one look at Mom's face, and I knew the discussion was over.

I reluctantly climbed the wooden stairs to my grandfather's room. As I knocked softly on the oak door, I wondered if I could still convince my mom into letting me go. Much to my astonishment, Grandpa unexpectedly whipped the door opened, startling me.

"Hi, Grandpa," I stammered, shuffling my feet. "I was just wondering . . . If you're not busy . . . um . . . if you'd like to do something together?"

"Sure! Why don't we go for a walk in the woods?" Grandpa exclaimed, grabbing his jacket.

Taking a walk in the woods would be about as much fun as watching paint dry, but I knew I wasn't going to get out of this. I was doomed to spend a boring afternoon in the woods.

"The woods harbor fascinating secrets. Why, did you know that you could survive foraging in the woods with nothing more than a flashlight and a tin cup?"

I looked up at Grandpa with a puzzled expression, but Grandpa just smiled.

GO ON →

We strolled along the woody path. Grandpa was like a jackrabbit, darting around from place to place, busily examining the plants that thrived abundantly in the brilliant midday sunshine. Stopping at an enormous blackberry bush that ran alongside the path, he began informing me about the plump berries that covered the branches.

Stifling a yawn, I shifted my weight from one foot to the next, and tried to look interested. "I know what blackberries are; Mom bought them at the supermarket all the time."

"Sure, you can purchase them at the grocery store, but they taste better in the wild. Did you know its prickly stem can be peeled and consumed, too?" Grandpa asked, as he plucked a few berries off the prickly branches and dropped them into my hands.

As soon as the sweet, delicious berries touched my tongue, my eyes widened. Grandpa was right, they were delicious!

"Are there other plants in the woods that could be eaten?" I asked, my stomach growling.

"Yes, all around you. However, not all plants are edible; some are poisonous and could make you sick, or worse."

"This is foxglove," he said, gesturing to a delicate, bell-shaped flower. "It is used to make digitalis, a medicine for people with heart disease." Then, in a somber tone, he warned. "If a healthy person ate it, it could make them very sick. Before you eat anything that is unfamiliar, it's very important to ask an adult."

As I cautiously examined the seemingly harmless plant, I began to wonder how Grandpa knew so many things about the woods.

"My grandfather taught me everything I know. Back then, people survived by living off the land, utilizing the resources around them."

GO ON →

"For example, the tree over here is a sassafras tree; it produces a nutrient-rich, dark blue fruit that smells like root beer. The bark can be used to make sassafras tea and, if you're camping, and really in a pinch, you can shred the tender twigs and use them as a toothbrush."

As I imagined what it would be like to use a twig as a toothbrush, Grandfather paused to examine a clump of dandelions growing next to a tree.

"Even the mischievous dandelion is edible," he said, plucking a bright yellow flower from the grass, twiddling it between his thumb and fingers. "My grandma used its jagged leaves and roots as a vegetable; they are high in vitamin A and C, and rich in calcium."

"What did they taste like?" I asked. I couldn't imagine eating the sticky flower that Dad had banished from the front lawn.

"They tasted like lettuce, but more bitter. I grew up with them; I didn't think too much about them. Some people put the yellow flowers in their salads, but most people look at dandelions as a weed."

Slowly, I surveyed the woods around me, as if I was seeing it for the very first time. "Wow, I had no idea the woods could be so exciting. This is cool!" Do you think we could take some dandelions home and have some with dinner? I pleaded.

"I don't see why not, my boy. Grab the hem of your shirt, and we can use it as a sack to carry them."

"This has been the best day ever! Just wait until I tell Ethan what he missed."

GO ON →

8 Read the sentence from the text.

I <u>reluctantly</u> climbed the wooden stairs to my grandfather's room.

Which word is a synonym of <u>reluctantly</u>?

(A) noisily

(B) carefully

(C) unwillingly

(D) shyly

9 How does Josh feel when Mom tells him to spend time with Grandpa? Select **two** options.

(A) "I stammered, shuffling my feet"

(B) "I knew I wasn't going to get out of this"

(C) "I looked up at Grandpa with a puzzled expression"

(D) "Stifling a yawn, I shifted my weight from one foot to the next"

(E) "I cautiously examined the seemingly harmless plant"

(F) "I couldn't imagine eating the sticky flower"

GO ON →

10 Read the sentence from the text.

Grandpa was <u>like a jackrabbit</u>, darting around from place to place, busily examining the plants that thrived abundantly in the brilliant midday sunshine.

Why does Josh use the simile "like a jackrabbit" to describe Grandpa?

(A) to show how excited Grandpa is to be exploring in the woods

(B) to show that Grandpa finds being in the woods overwhelming

(C) to show that Grandpa likes to study animals as well as plants

(D) to show that Grandpa is confused by his surroundings

11 The following question has two parts. First, answer part A. Then, answer part B.

Part A: Read the sentences from the text.

"Are there other plants in the woods that could be eaten?" I asked, my stomach growling.

"Yes, all around you. However, not all plants are edible; some are poisonous and could make you sick, or worse."

What does edible mean?

(A) good tasting

(B) pretty to see

(C) safe to eat

(D) well known

Part B: Which phrase from the sentences **best** explains your answer in part A?

(A) "could be eaten"

(B) "my stomach growling"

(C) "not all plants"

(D) "make you sick"

GO ON →

12 The following question has two parts. First, answer part A. Then, answer part B.

Part A: What is the theme of the text?

(A) Things are not always what we expect.

(B) It's important to respect your elders.

(C) We can't always do what we want to do.

(D) Nature can be dangerous.

Part B: Which sentence from the text **best** supports your answer in part A?

(A) "'But, Mom,' I whined. 'He never wants to do anything interesting.'"

(B) "However, one look at Mom's face, and I knew the discussion was over."

(C) "'Before you eat anything that is unfamiliar, it's very important to ask an adult.'"

(D) "'This has been the best day ever! Just wait until I tell Ethan what he missed.'"

GO ON →

13 The following question has two parts. First, answer part A. Then, answer part B.

Part A: How does the point of view of the text help the reader better understand Josh's feelings?

(A) by reporting everything he says

(B) by showing what he is thinking

(C) by describing his actions toward others

(D) by explaining how people react to him

Part B: Which phrase from the text supports your answer in part A?

(A) "whipped the door open"

(B) "'like to do something together'"

(C) "doomed to spend a boring afternoon"

(D) "but Grandpa just smiled"

GO ON →

14 How do the narrator's feelings about spending time with his grandfather change? Use evidence from the text to explain your answer.

_____

_____

_____

_____

_____

GO ON →

Read the texts. Then answer the questions.

Stormalong Disobeys an Order

Have you ever heard of Old Stormalong, the greatest sailor of all time? He was so strong that he could win an arm wrestling contest with an octopus with one arm tied behind his back. He was so tall that he used the ship's mast for a hat rack. And whenever the wind died down and becalmed the ship, Stormalong would take a seat at the stern and start whistling. With just one tune, he would puff out enough air to keep the ship sailing until the breeze picked up again. As you can imagine, ship captains loved having Stormalong aboard, even if it did require an extra supply room just to keep him fed.

When he was a lad, Stormalong was of course quite big for his age. He was also as curious as a monkey and as lively as a grasshopper. This was a challenging combination for his parents. They had to work hard to keep little Stormy out of mischief. Every day, they took him to the beach in hopes of wearing him out. Stormy would run up and down chasing seagulls. Scooping up sea creatures in his bucket, he would examine them awhile and then let them go. Most of the animals seemed okay with this. The giant squids, however, grew tired of the game and took off for the deepest parts of the ocean. They stayed there so long that folks started to doubt they really existed.

There are a lot of good yarns about Stormalong. One about his teenage years has Stormy and his friends doing "cannonballs" from a diving raft. They were trying to make the biggest splash. On Stormy's first turn, he leaped out over the water, hugged his knees to his chest, and curled his body into a ball. His splash was HUGE! In fact, the spray created the Great Lakes. The ripples formed the currents that still circle through the oceans today.

One of the best stories comes from the summer Stormy's parents signed him up for sailing lessons. He loved zipping through the water with the salt spray in his face. Ignoring his instructor's warnings about going too fast, he once crashed right into Africa. He hit the continent so hard that a piece broke off and formed Australia. Of course, his sailboat was destroyed. Luckily, Stormy was a true fish when it came to swimming. He just headed back across the ocean, using the opportunity to practice his crawl stroke. He arrived home in time for dinner and wasn't even tired.

GO ON →

When he was 18, Stormalong decided to become a sailor. He kissed his parents goodbye and set off for the nearest seaport. The captain saw him coming from two states away and signed him up before he even arrived. Though some in the crew were doubtful about his lack of experience, Stormalong promptly proved his worth.

Before the Panama Canal was built, ships traveling between the Atlantic and the Pacific had to sail around the tip of South America. It was a long and extremely dangerous journey. On his very first voyage, Stormalong's ship was set to sail that route. Stormalong had lookout duty. He spotted some bad weather, a huge storm near the Falkland Islands. Going through the storm would mean certain disaster for the ship. However, the first mate refused to tell the captain, who was asleep in his cabin. "You can't see the Falklands from here," he scoffed. "Get back to your post."

What could Stormalong do? Disobeying orders was a serious offense. He'd likely be severely punished. Even worse, he'd probably never get hired on a ship again. If he did obey the order, his shipmates might perish. Stormalong made his decision. He didn't go back to his post. Instead, he jumped overboard, picked up the vessel, hoisted it over Panama, and dropped it into the Pacific. The splash woke the captain. He was not angry at all about Stormalong taking matters into his own hands. In fact, he fired the first mate and offered Stormalong the job. (He also began promoting the idea of a canal across Panama.)

Saving that ship made Stormalong an instant legend. People still tell stories about him to this day.

GO ON →

Read the text "The Poet and the General." Then answer the questions.

The Poet and the General

CHARACTERS

NARRATOR	
JOHN WHEATLEY	wealthy merchant, white, age 58
YOUNG PHILLIS	girl, black, age 7
MARY WHEATLEY	John's daughter, white, age 18
PHILLIS WHEATLEY	woman, black, age 23
GEORGE WASHINGTON	man, white, age 44
OFFICER	man, any age

SCENE 1

NARRATOR: (*Spotlighted on dark stage*) In October 1775, early in the Revolutionary War, a young woman named Phillis Wheatley sent a poem to General George Washington. In a letter dated February 28, 1776, Washington invited Wheatley, who lived in Boston, Massachusetts, to visit him at his headquarters in nearby Cambridge. She reportedly did so in March 1776, but no one knows for sure. The poet and the general—what might such a meeting have been like?

Narrator walks offstage. The light dims.

SCENE 2

SETTING: The parlor of the Wheatley home in Boston, 1761.
Mary Wheatley is sitting and sewing when John Wheatley and Young Phillis enter from the left.

JOHN WHEATLEY: Mary, this child has just arrived from Africa aboard Captain Fitch's vessel. I bought her to be a servant and companion to your mother. She speaks no English but seems very intelligent and quick to learn. Perhaps you can teach her?

GO ON →

MARY WHEATLEY: I will happily do so, Father. What is the child's name?

JOHN WHEATLEY: She is called Phillis, after the ship on which she arrived.

MARY WHEATLEY: Phillis—Phillis Wheatley. It's a good name. Come with me, Phillis Wheatley.

She takes the child's hand and leads her from the room. The lights dim.

SCENE 3

SETTING: The dining room of a house, March 1776.
General Washington sips a cup of tea and examines some papers on the table.
There is a knock at the door.

OFFICER: (*From offstage.*) General Washington, Phillis Wheatley has arrived.

Phillis Wheatley now age 23, enters from the right. General
Washington stands and gestures for her to sit, then takes his seat.

WASHINGTON: You are a remarkable woman, Mistress Wheatley. I am flattered you have chosen me as the subject of one of your poems, though I would quarrel with the title: "His Excellency George Washington." I am no "Excellency"—just a man serving his country.

WHEATLEY: I meant no offense, sir. The title merely reflects the judgments I hear spoken all around me. Your fellow citizens think very highly of you, General.

WASHINGTON: I wonder what the state of their opinion will be as this war with England continues. They may feel I have led them out of the frying pan into the fire.

WHEATLEY: Sir, all praise is rightly deserved. Your past achievements—your bravery, honesty, manners, intelligence—are well known. They are the reason the people confidently call on you to lead the brave troops who protect us and gain us our freedom from English tyrants.

GO ON →

WASHINGTON:	You say the same in your poem. I thank you for those elegant words. But I am curious, how did you come to write poetry? How were you educated?
WHEATLEY:	After I learned English, Mary Wheatley taught me to read and write. Since the age of 12, I have been reading English and Latin poets. The Wheatleys have always encouraged me. They even help me publish my poems.
WASHINGTON:	Ah, yes, I have seen your book, *Poems on Various Subjects, Religious and Moral*. I understand that yours is only the second book published by a woman from the American colonies. That is quite an achievement for any person so young, and especially one who has lived in enslavement. (Stands) I am honored to have met you, Mistress Wheatley, but I regret I must now return to my work.
WHEATLEY:	*(rises and curtseys)* General, you have many unencouraging days ahead. When times are hardest, take comfort in the saying that "the hour is darkest before the dawn."
WASHINGTON:	You have succeeded in rising above the tyranny of slavery. That gives me great hope in our struggle with the tyranny of England.

Washington grasps Wheatley's hand in both of his. The lights dim.

GO ON →

Answer these questions about "Stormalong Disobeys an Order."

15 Read the sentence from the text.

Luckily, <u>Stormy was a true fish</u> when it came to swimming.

What does the metaphor "Stormy was a true fish" mean in the sentence above?

Ⓐ Stormy used fins to swim.

Ⓑ Stormy was a very skillful swimmer.

Ⓒ Stormy learned to swim by observing fish.

Ⓓ Stormy could swim underwater for a long time.

16 Which details from the text are examples of hyperbole? Select **all** that apply.

Ⓐ Disobeying orders was a serious offense.

Ⓑ Stormy's whistling could keep a ship sailing when there was no wind.

Ⓒ Stormalong's parents had to work hard to keep him out of mischief.

Ⓓ Stormy's cannonball splash created the Great Lakes and ocean currents.

Ⓔ Stormalong kissed his parents goodbye and set off for the nearest seaport.

Ⓕ Stormy crashed his sailboat into Africa and created the continent of Australia.

GO ON →

17 Stormalong has to make a hard decision, and either choice he makes will cause problems. What leads up to the decision, and what lesson does he learn? Use at least **two** details from the text to support your answer.

_____

_____

_____

_____

_____

_____

GO ON →

Name: _____ Date: _____

Answer these questions about "The Poet and the General."

18 Explain how the settings and stage directions for each scene help the reader better understand the play. Support your answer with details from the text.

_____

_____

_____

_____

_____

19 George Washington describes Phillis Wheatly as "a remarkable woman." Select **two** statements that **best** support his point of view.

(A) She was named after a ship.

(B) She used flattering words to describe others.

(C) She believed Washington would be a great leader.

(D) She arrived in America as a small child.

(E) She began reading Latin poetry when she was only 12.

(F) She published poems while she was an enslaved person.

20 Read the line from the play.

They may feel I have led them <u>out of the frying pan into the fire.</u>

What does the saying "out of the frying pan into the fire" mean?

(A) from the kitchen into another room

(B) from a place of safety into a place of danger

(C) from one bad situation into a worse situation

(D) from an uncertainty into a definite course of action

GO ON →

Now answer these questions about "Stormalong Disobeys an Order" and "The Poet and the General."

21 Compare and contrast Phillis Wheatley's view of George Washington with the tall tale narrator's view of Stormalong. Use examples from **both** texts to explain the basis for their feelings and the ways they express them.

_____

_____

_____

_____

_____

_____

_____

_____

_____

_____

_____

_____

_____

_____

_____

_____

GO ON →

The text below needs revision. Read the text. Then answer the questions.

Dolley Payne Todd Madison (1768–1849) was not the first First Lady, but she _____(1)_____ the first to take on many of the roles that First Ladies still play today. _____(2)_____ husband James was the fourth President of the United States. Throughout Madison's time in office, Dolley worked hard to make foreign officials feel welcome in the White House. She wanted to show _____(3)_____ that we Americans were not rough country folk. Our education and manners were equal to _____(4)_____ in Europe. Social events also gave Dolley the chance to help her husband with his job. She used them to gain information that might be useful. She even persuaded some guests to change _____(5)_____ views of Madison's policies.

Modern First Ladies often dedicate _____(6)_____ to particular public projects. They _____(7)_____ programs to support literacy, for example, or improve the nation's health. Dolley Madison was the first to do this. She organized a home for orphan girls in Washington, D.C., and donated food for _____(8)_____ kitchen.

During the War of 1812, the British army burned the White House. Dolley refused to leave without a large portrait of George Washington, _____(9)_____ hung in the State Dining Room. This was a very patriotic act. Fortunately, no other First Lady has needed to repeat _____(10)_____ !

GO ON →

22 Which answer should go in blank (1)?

(A) were

(B) was

(C) are

23 Which answer should go in blank (2)?

(A) She's

(B) Hers

(C) Her

24 Which answer should go in blank (3)?

(A) her

(B) him

(C) them

25 Which answer should go in blank (4)?

(A) anyones

(B) anyone's

(C) anyones'

26 Which answer should go in blank (5)?

(A) their

(B) there

(C) they're

GO ON →

27 Which answer should go in blank (6)?

   Ⓐ theirself

   Ⓑ themselfs

   Ⓒ themselves

28 Which answer should go in blank (7)?

   Ⓐ start

   Ⓑ starts

   Ⓒ starting

29 Which answer should go in blank (8)?

   Ⓐ it's

   Ⓑ its

   Ⓒ its's

30 Which answer should go in blank (9)?

   Ⓐ what

   Ⓑ who

   Ⓒ which

31 Which answer should go in blank (10)?

   Ⓐ it

   Ⓑ them

   Ⓒ those

STOP

Narrative Performance Task

Task:

Your class has been learning about how people decide what is important. Now the local newspaper is having a creative writing contest. Your teacher has asked each student in your class to write a narrative story for the contest about how they would communicate with a new student from another country.

Before you begin working on your story, you will do some research by reading two articles about different types of communication. After you have reviewed these sources, you will answer some questions about them. Briefly scan the sources and the three questions that follow. Then go back and read the sources carefully to gain the information you will need to answer the questions and finalize your research. You may take notes on the information you find in the sources as you read. Your notes will be available to you as you read.

Directions for Part 1

You will now examine two sources. You can re-examine any of the sources as often as you like.

Research Questions:

After examining the sources, use the remaining time in Part 1 to answer three questions about them. Your answers to these questions will be scored. Also, your answers will help you think about the information you have read and viewed, which should help you write your story. You may look at your notes when you think it would be helpful. Answer the questions in the spaces provided.

GO ON →

Source #1: A Language of Dots

Ten- year-old Louis Braille felt a shiver of excitement as he rode in the stagecoach. He was on his way to the Royal Institute for Blind Youth in Paris, France. At that time, in 1819, it was the first and only school for blind children like him. Louis eagerly awaited his chance to learn subjects like history, science, and geography. The institute had special books with raised texts he could read with his fingers.

Disappointing Discoveries

Sadly, the institute's large, heavy books were awkward to handle and challenging to decode. Louis had to carefully trace the bumpy outline of each big letter with his finger, one at a time, to read a word. Some of the letters had similar shapes and were difficult to distinguish.

Furthermore, the school's library only contained three volumes. Few companies published the expensive books with raised letters. Louis felt frustrated; he began to search for a better way for blind people to communicate through writing. The ability to read and record information would enable them to be better educated and more independent.

Night Writing

Several years later, a French army captain visited the school. He told students about a code he invented called "night-writing." With his system, soldiers punched a series of raised dots and dashes into cardboard. The different marks stood for the syllables in words. Using the code, he could send brief messages to his soldiers during the night. The soldiers could read them with their fingers, so they did not need to light lanterns that enemies might notice.

In a flash, Louis realized the captain's style of writing would work well for blind people. They could read dots much easier with their fingers than big letters. However, the captain's codes were too long; some of the syllables required twenty dots and took too long to decode. In addition, there were no signs to tell readers when sentences began and ended, which was confusing.

GO ON →

A Cell of Dots

For the next three years, fourteen-year-old Louis devoted himself to perfecting his own "raised dot alphabet." After experimenting, he decided to use a rectangular cell of six dots to form his letters. Different combinations of the dots represented certain letters. For instance, two raised dots at the top of the cell represented the letter "c."

Louis's new alphabet offered definite advantages to "touch" readers. The small cells quickly glided under their fingertips. As a result, they could conveniently slide their hand straight across the page and read more swiftly than before.

Louis's new system also included rules to make sentences easier to interpret. For instance, a dot in the bottom right corner signaled that the next letter was a capital. Plus, Louis designed individual symbols for punctuation marks, so readers could correctly group words.

Helpful Shortcuts

As Louis developed his language, he expanded it to include certain symbols that stood for groups of letters or short words. For instance, there was a specific symbol for "ing" and another specific symbol for the word "and." Other shortcuts, like using the letters "sd" to mean "said," soon became popular, too.

Today, people throughout the world use the Braille alphabet. It includes notations for letters, words, numbers and musical notes. You may spy the dots in public places, like elevators. Thanks to Louis, people can gain valuable knowledge with the brush of their fingertips.

©Christopher Stubbs/Alamy

GO ON →

Source #2: Talking Leaves for the Cherokee

Sequoyah stared in amazement as his fellow soldiers read their letters from home. The idea of using marks on a paper to communicate with others captivated him. Sequoyah belonged to the Cherokee people, and Native Americans had no written language. When Sequoyah completed his military service, he remembered the white man's "talking leaves.

A Bold Decision

Sequoyah married and had a family, carrying on his mother's business as a trader. Later, he trained himself to be a blacksmith and a silversmith. Because Sequoyah had a lame leg which limited his physical abilities, working as a craftsman suited him.

Whenever possible, Sequoyah devoted his time to his cherished dream; he intended to create a written Cherokee language. Many of his friends and acquaintances thought Sequoyah was foolish. They criticized him for wasting his days, but Sequoyah ignored their comments. He hoped to give the Cherokee a way to communicate their thoughts on paper and to record their nation's history.

The First Attempt

Sequoyah had no experience with any written language, but he understood that the mysterious marks on the soldiers' letters had represented spoken words. At first, Sequoyah started making a different symbol to represent every known Cherokee word, carving the characters into bark with his knife. His collection grew at a furious rate until there were over a thousand characters.

Frustrated, Sequoyah realized his system would not work. People could never memorize that many symbols. However, Sequoyah's efforts were not a complete failure; he became an expert at understanding his musical, flowing language. In the process, he recognized that words contained consonant sounds followed by vowel sounds, or distinct syllables.

GO ON →

A Syllabary

Next, Sequoyah focused his attention on inventing symbols for every syllable sound in his language. Some historical accounts say Sequoyah used the letters and numbers from an old English spelling book as models for his symbols. However, to Sequoyah, the letter "S" was just a snake shape. He did not know that in the English language it represented a hissing sound. In addition, he turned some of the letter symbols upside down or sideways.

Determined, Sequoyah worked tirelessly to perfect and limit the symbols in his syllabary. In the end, he divided the sounds of his language into 85 syllables. Sequoyah felt that people would be able to read, write, and memorize that amount.

A New World Opens

When Sequoyah announced that he had successfully invented a written Cherokee language, people scoffed at him. To prove the truth, Sequoyah convinced an important chief to write a letter to a friend using the syllabary and to seal the message in an envelope. Next, Sequoyah brought the letter to the friend and broke open the wax seal. In front of a doubtful crowd of Cherokee leaders, he handed the letter to his daughter and asked her to read it aloud.

Ahyokah, who had often been her father's assistant, did so without a pause. The Cherokee leaders were stunned and impressed; they wisely understood how valuable the "picture talk" could be to their nation. Before long, the leaders worked to acquire a printing press. In time, their nation printed the first Native American newspaper.

Today, Sequoyah's syllabary remains in active use. In fact, some computer search engines and cell phones have created keyboards with its symbols for their users. The symbols once carved in bark now connect people through wireless technology.

GO ON →

1 Read the paragraph from Source #2.

Whenever possible, Sequoyah devoted his time to his cherished dream; he intended to create a written Cherokee language. Many of his friends and acquaintances thought Sequoyah was foolish. They criticized him for wasting his days, but Sequoyah ignored their comments. He hoped to give the Cherokee a way to communicate their thoughts on paper and to record their nation's history.

How does this information about Sequoyah help the reader understand the work of Louis Braille in Source #2? Select **two** options.

(A) Braille wanted to share the story about schools for the blind.

(B) Braille wanted an easier way for the blind to be able to read.

(C) Braille wished to help the French soldiers share information.

(D) Braille invested a lot of time to achieve his goal to help the blind.

(E) Braille's raised-dot alphabet was not so effective as raised letters.

(F) Braille felt that most people did not understand how to read by touch.

GO ON →

2 Describe how the information in the sources helps the reader better understand the different ways people can communicate. Use **two** details from the sources to support your explanation. For each detail, include the source title or number.

_____

_____

_____

_____

_____

3 Explain how the sources show the importance of persistence. Give at least **two** reasons, **one** from Source #1 and **one** from Source #2, to support your explanation. For each reason, include the source title or number.

_____

_____

_____

_____

_____

_____

GO ON →

Directions for Part 2

You will now review your notes and sources, and plan, draft, and edit your narrative story. You may use your notes to refer to the sources.

Now read your assignment and the information about how the story will be scored; then begin your work.

Your Assignment:

The local newspaper is having a writing contest. The topic is about how you would communicate with someone who speaks your language. The audience for your story is your teacher, the editor of the newspaper, and the community. The winning entry will be published in the local newspaper.

Now, you are going to write a narrative story to submit to your teacher. For your story, imagine a new student has just enrolled in your school. The student is from a foreign country and does not speak any English. Your teacher has asked you to help the student feel welcome by learning how to communicate with the rest of the students. In your story, describe how you develop a way to communicate. The story should be several paragraphs long.

Writers often do research to add realistic details to the setting, characters, and plot in their stories. When writing your story, find ways to incorporate information and details from the sources. Make sure you develop your characters, the setting, and the plot. Use details, dialogue, and description where appropriate.

REMEMBER: A well-written narrative story

- is well-organized and stays on topic
- has an introduction and conclusion
- uses details from the sources
- develops ideas fully
- uses clear language
- follows rules of writing (spelling, punctuation, and grammar)

Now begin work on your narrative story. Manage your time carefully so that you can plan, write, revise, and edit the final draft of your narrative story. Write your response on a separate sheet of paper.

Answer Key

Name: _____

Question	Correct Answer	Content Focus	CCSS	Complexity
1	see below	Synonyms and Antonyms	L.5.5c	DOK 2
2	C, E	Author's Point of View	RI.5.8	DOK 3
3A	A	Context Clues: Definitions and Restatements	L.5.4.a	DOK 2
3B	B	Context Clues: Definitions and Restatements/Text Evidence	L.5.4a/ RL.5.1	DOK 2
4	D, E	Text Features: Photographs and Illustrations	RI.4.7	DOK 2
5	A	Synonyms and Antonyms	L.5.5c	DOK 2
6	B	Text Features: Chart	RI.4.7	DOK 2
7	see below	Author's Point of View	RI.5.8	DOK 3
8	C	Synonyms and Antonyms	L.5.5c	DOK 2
9	B, D	Point of View	RL.5.6	DOK 2
10	A	Similes	L.5.5a	DOK 2
11A	C	Context Clues: Definitions and Restatements	L.5.4a	DOK 3
11B	A	Context Clues: Definitions and Restatements/Text Evidence	L.5.4a/ RL.5.1	DOK 3
12A	A	Theme	RL.5.2	DOK 3
12B	D	Theme/Text Evidence	RL.5.2/ RL5.1	DOK 3
13A	B	Point of View	RL.5.6	DOK 3
13B	C	Text Evidence	RL.5.6/ RL.5.1	DOK 3
14	see below	Point of View	RL.5.6	DOK 3
15	B	Metaphor	L.5.5a	DOK 2
16	B, D, F	Hyperbole	RL.5.4	DOK 2
17	see below	Theme	RL5.2	DOK 3
18	see below	Text Features: Stage Directions and Scenes	RL.5.3	DOK 2
19	E, F	Point of View	RL.5.6	DOK 3
20	C	Adages and Proverbs	L.5.5b	DOK 2
21	see below	Compare Across Texts	RL.5.9	DOK 4

156

Grade 5 • Unit Assessment • Unit 4

Copyright © McGraw-Hill Education

Answer Key

Name: _____

Question	Correct Answer	Content Focus	CCSS	Complexity
22	B	Pronoun-Verb Agreement	L.5.2	DOK 1
23	C	Possessive Pronouns	L.5.2	DOK 1
24	C	Pronouns and Antecedents	L.3.1f	DOK 1
25	B	Possessive Pronouns	L.5.2	DOK 1
26	A	Pronouns and Homophones	L.4.1g	DOK 1
27	C	Kinds of Pronouns	L.3.1a	DOK 1
28	A	Pronoun-Verb Agreement	L.5.2	DOK 1
29	B	Pronouns and Homophones	L.4.1g	DOK 1
30	C	Kinds of Pronouns	L.3.1a	DOK 1
31	A	Pronouns and Antecedents	L.3.1f	DOK 1

Comprehension: Selected Responses 2, 4, 6, 9, 12A, 12B, 13A, 13B, 16, 19, 20	/18	%
Comprehension: Constructed Response 7, 14, 17, 18, 21	/12	%
Vocabulary 1, 3A, 3B, 5, 8, 10, 11A, 11B, 15	/14	%
English Language Conventions 22–31	/10	%
Total Unit Assessment Score	/54	%

1. Students should match the following:
   - disease: illness
   - cure: treatment
   - modern: current

7. **2-point response:** The author believes that modern medicine "has helped people survive serious diseases and suffer less pain." The author also explains that many medicines used today come from plants used in folk medicine a long time ago. For example, malaria is treated today with quinine. Quinine comes from the folk medicine cinchona powder.

14. **2-point response:** At the beginning of the story, Josh does not want to spend time with his grandfather. When his grandfather suggests walking in the woods, he goes along, but knows he will not have any fun. Josh tries to fake excitement. However, as his grandfather reveals all of the secrets of the woods, Josh begins to see the woods differently. By the end of the story, he is excited to share his new knowledge with his friend, Ethan.

17. **2-point response:** When the first mate orders Stormalong to return to his post he wants to obey, but he is afraid everyone will perish if he does. He knows that if he refuses to go back to his post, he can save everyone's lives, but he will risk this job and future ones. He chooses to disobey the first mate. Stormalong lifts the ship from one ocean to another to avoid the storm, and he saves the ship and crew. He learns that sometimes you have to break a rule to do something good.

18 **2-point response:** The settings and stage directions for each scene provide information that is not always apparent from the characters' dialogue. They help the reader visualize where the play takes place and they make it easier to understand the action of the play

21 **4-point response:** Wheatley and the narrator both base their points of view at least in part on what other people have said. Both use special names that reflect their feelings (His Excellency, Sir, Old Stormalong, Stormy). Both refer to the subject's past achievements. Wheatley respects Washington, while the narrator is amused by Stormalong. Wheatley speaks broadly of Washington's successes, without mentioning actual deeds or events. The narrator describes specific episodes and includes some of Stormalong's mishaps as well. Wheatley expresses her admiration in written form (a poem) and in person; the narrator's feelings come through indirectly during the narrative. Wheatley speaks in general terms but does not describe actual deeds or events; the narrator describes specific episodes.

Narrative Performance Task				
Question	Answer	CCSS	Complexity	Score
1	B, D	RI.5.1, RI.5.2, RI.5.7, RI.5.8, RI.5.9 W.5.2, W.5.3a-e, W.5.4, W.5.7 L.5.1, L.5.2	DOK 2	/1
2	see below		DOK 3	/2
3	see below		DOK 3	/2
Narrative Story	see below		DOK 4	/4 [P/O] /4 [D/E] /2 [C]
Total Score				/15

2 **2-point response:** Source #1 discusses Braille, a system using raised dots to represent letters. This form of communication allows people who are blind to use their fingertips to learn information from books and to communicate in written form.

Source #2 describes an alphabet that was developed using pictures to represent the sounds and syllables of the Cherokee language. In the past, the Cherokee people were only able to communicate verbally. This new development allowed them to communicate using written language.

3 **2-point response:** In Source #1, Louis Braille set out to develop a better way for blind people to communicate through writing. He spent many years trying to develop a system that was easy to use and to understand. His first attempt, using "night-writing," was difficult to read and confusing. However, because he never gave up, people with sight disabilities today can communicate using the Braille system that he developed.

In Source #2, Sequoyah wished to give the Cherokee people a way to communicate with others and to record their history. His initial attempt at using symbols to represent Cherokee words ended in failure. Even when his friends told him to, he refused to give up on his idea. Eventually, his efforts led to the development of the first Native-American newspaper.

10-point anchor paper: I was sitting at my desk, waiting for the bell to ring on a sluggish Monday morning when I noticed a girl with long blonde hair standing in the doorway. Glancing at her quickly, I recalled seeing her picture in the local paper. She was the daughter of a visiting musician from Russia who was spending the next year working at the university. I smiled and waved at her, thinking how frightening it must be to walk into a room filled with strangers. She smiled back and walked toward me.

"Hi! Would you like to sit beside me? Here is an empty desk." I offered. "My name is Sally. I read about your family in the newspaper last week." I said slowly and clearly.

She just smiled in return.

Deciding that I needed to try something different, I took a piece of paper and wrote my name, adding an arrow beside it that pointed at me. She responded by taking out a pencil, writing a word, and drawing an arrow too.

"It is nice to meet you, Alina!" I said.

Mr. Schuester walked into the classroom and science class began. He noticed that Alina was sitting in the vacant chair, so he asked her if she would like to introduce herself to the class. Smiling, she walked to the front of the room, carrying the piece of paper. She held it up and said, "Alina."

Mr. Schuester recognized, as we all did, that Alina did not speak English. He called the office to request assistance, and soon Mrs. Johansen, an English as a Second Language teacher arrived in our classroom. Mrs. Johansen is my mom's best friend, so I was quick to fill her in on what I remembered reading in the newspaper.

"I think that your attempt to be friends with Alina will be so very helpful, Sally. She knows that you will do whatever it takes to communicate with her. Would you consider being her language mentor?" Mrs. Johansen asked.

"Sure," I agreed.

Alina and I worked together during study hall and after school. We practiced with flash cards and with programs on the computer. Sometimes we even listened to children's nursery songs in her language so that she could practice translating them into English.

Weeks and months flew by. Without really working hard, I had managed to learn Russian while teaching Alina my language. We both laughed when I told Alina that I had even had a dream where everyone was speaking in Russian!

When Alina's father's position at the university ended, we were quite sad. We made a promise to video chat every week so that we could practice our new language skills. We also decided to e-mail each other in the native language of the receiver and answer in the opposite language. We both were determined to not only keep our friendship alive, but also to continue to build our language skills.

Three years have passed, and we still continue our weekly video chats in both languages. My best friend may be thousands of miles away from me, but technology keeps us close.

Read the text. Then answer the questions.

Going to the Doctor

If you go to a doctor's office today, the doctor will usually know the cause of your illness and how to treat it. That was not true of doctors 200 years ago. No matter what symptoms you had, the treatment would be the same. Doctors did the best they could with what they knew at the time, but their knowledge was limited. The practice of medicine has changed a lot since then, both in understanding what causes diseases and knowing how to treat them.

In the 1700s, doctors believed that people's bodies held four fluids called "humors." These matched the elements of the natural world: air, water, earth, and fire. The four humors had to be balanced for a person to be healthy. One of these four was blood. Doctors believed that a person who had too much "bad blood" would become sick, and the best way to keep people healthy or to cure a problem was to get rid of the bad blood.

For hundreds of years, doctors used bloodletting to treat patients with any number of problems, from fevers to back pain to broken bones. To remove the "bad blood," a doctor made a small cut in an arm or near a wound. The doctor then collected some amount of blood in a bowl. In most cases, the doctor would continue the bleeding until the patient was close to passing out. People believed this would get rid of the bad blood so that the patient's body could become balanced again.

The practice was so common that most doctors carried bloodletting pouches and kits with them. These kits contained tools for making small cuts, but people who didn't want to go to the doctor for bloodletting could go to a barber instead. Barbers performed the same procedure on people to help them stay healthy. The emblem for a barber shop was a red and white striped pole. Red represented blood, and white was for the bandages used to stop the bleeding.

George Washington died in 1799 from what modern doctors think was a throat infection. Like most people at the time, he believed in bloodletting, and asked to be bled when he became very sick with a sore throat. During his brief illness, doctors drained a lot of blood from his body. They hoped it would cure him, but it did not; Washington died twenty-four hours later. Bloodletting probably did not kill him, but it certainly did not help him recover.

GO ON →

In the early 1800s, if a person was injured, a doctor might perform surgery. This could involve cutting off an arm or leg that was badly injured and could not be saved, or removing a bullet or other object from a wound. In those days, more people died from surgery than were saved.

One of the reasons so many people died then was that doctors did not know about bacteria. They did not clean the germs from their hands or medical tools between treating patients. Many patients got infections and died, but doctors did not understand the real cause of death.

In 1867, British surgeon Joseph Lister determined that carefully cleaning hands, medical equipment, and wounds could greatly reduce the risk of infections, but American doctors were slow to accept his views. It was the treatment of another American President that helped change their minds.

In 1881, President James Garfield was shot as he entered a train station. Doctors tried to remove the bullet. However, they did not clean their hands or tools. They tended to him for about ten weeks before he died. Doctors found that he died from an infection rather than from the bullet. That discovery helped bring about some important changes in medicine.

Today, doctors know much more than they did in the past and use the best information available. We are lucky that modern medicine is as advanced as it is, and offers so many benefits. Even so, some of their methods may change someday, as scientists make new discoveries.

GO ON →

1 The following question has two parts. First, answer part A. Then, answer part B.

Part A: Read these sentences from the first paragraph of the text.

No matter what <u>symptoms</u> you had, the treatment would be the same. Doctors did the best they could with what they knew at the time, but their knowledge was limited. The practice of medicine has changed a lot since then, both in understanding what causes diseases and knowing how to treat them.

What does <u>symptoms</u> mean?

(A) types of work

(B) ways to explain

(C) signs of a disease

(D) members of a family

Part B: Which phrase from the sentences **best** supports your answer in part A?

(A) "knowledge was limited"

(B) "practice of medicine"

(C) "what causes diseases"

(D) "would be the same"

GO ON →

2 Read the sentence from the text.

Barbers performed the same <u>procedure</u> on people to help them stay healthy.

The word <u>procedure</u> has Latin roots that mean "go forward." Which phrase **best** defines <u>procedure</u>? Choose **two** options.

(A) a future plan

(B) a course of action

(C) a list of questions

(D) a series of steps

(E) a point of view

(F) a sharp tool

3 Read the paragraph from the text.

One of the reasons so many people died then was that doctors did not know about <u>bacteria</u>. They did not clean the germs from their hands or medical tools between treating patients. Many patients got infections and died, but doctors did not understand the real cause of death.

Which phrase from the paragraph helps the reader understand what <u>bacteria</u> means?

(A) "One of the reasons"

(B) "clean the germs"

(C) "hands or medical tools"

(D) "Many patients"

GO ON →

4 Explain why doctors long ago used bloodletting to treat their patients. Use text evidence to support your answer.

_____

_____

_____

_____

_____

_____

5 The following question has two parts. First, answer part A. Then, answer part B.

Part A: How does the author organize the structure of the paragraph about President Garfield?

Ⓐ by showing that studying an error caused progress in medicine

Ⓑ by describing medical procedures with many details

Ⓒ by comparing and contrasting the surgeries of various Presidents

Ⓓ by showing how doctors lacked the tools for surgery

Part B: Which sentence from the text **best** supports your answer in part A?

Ⓐ "In 1881; President James Garfield was shot as he entered a train station."

Ⓑ "Doctors found that he died from an infection rather than from the bullet."

Ⓒ "They tended to him for about ten weeks before he died."

Ⓓ "Doctors tried to remove the bullet."

GO ON →

6 The author would **most likely** agree with which statements? Choose **two** options.

(A) Surgery in the 1800s is not much different than surgery today.

(B) Longer bloodletting might have saved Washington's life.

(C) Barbers were probably as successful at bloodletting as doctors.

(D) President Washington did not understand much about medicine.

(E) Medical procedures probably will not change much in the future.

(F) President Garfield might have survived if American doctors had used Joseph Lister's ideas.

7 The following question has two parts. First, answer part A. Then, answer part B.

Part A: How are the doctors from the 1700s and modern doctors similar?

(A) They use the best medical information available at the time.

(B) They believe that a person can have too much "bad blood."

(C) They understand that it is important to clean their tools.

(D) They do not always do what the patient wants.

Part B: Which detail from the text **best** supports your answer in part A?

(A) "carefully cleaning hands"

(B) "had to be balanced for a person to be healthy"

(C) "did the best they could with what they knew"

(D) "asked to be bled when he became very sick"

Read the text. Then answer the questions.

Jumping In

I stared at the framed photograph displayed on the desk in front of me. In the picture, I was wandering down a pebbled beach next to an enormous lake. When I closed my eyes, I could imagine the lake's icy fingers lapping at my feet and hear the screech of seagulls soaring overhead. I could feel the lake's fresh breeze tugging playfully at my shirt and smell the towering pines that guarded the shoreline.

However, when I glanced out my window, a drastically different world appeared. My father had accepted a teaching job in a small town on the western prairie, and we were living on a cattle ranch. Its sea of lonely fields stretched endlessly to the horizon, and, in the distance, I saw nothing but a few black smudges, which were grazing cows. A dusty road wound through the scene like an aimless line in a maze, and I wished that road could take me back to my beautiful lake home.

"Devon, Alicia's here," my dad announced, peering into my bedroom. "She's invited you to go bike riding."

I shrugged and quietly adjusted the swimming trophy that stood next to my photograph. Last spring, I had won first place in the crawl stroke contest at our club meet.

"I'll tell her you're coming," Dad declared firmly. "You've been moping in your room long enough."

Halfheartedly, I pushed back my desk chair and followed my father into the kitchen. Alicia was standing by the doorway, and she greeted me with an enthusiastic smile. She was excited to have someone her age move onto her family's ranch. They had built a new brick home, and we were renting the wooden cabin that stood next to it.

Five minutes later, Alicia and I were silently pedaling our bikes over a rough, gravel road that snaked toward the top of a nearby hill. The sun watched us, blazing in the sky, its punishing rays beating down on our backs. I stopped to rest, mopping my sweaty forehead with my hand.

"I wish we had a shady, wooded trail to ride on. There's nothing, not a tree or even a bush for miles," I grumbled, gazing at the desolate landscape, with nothing to see for miles. Suddenly, I noticed a sparkling blue pond nestled between some gentle hills. "Can we swim in that water?" I asked eagerly.

GO ON →

"It's a stock dam for the cattle to drink from," Alicia explained. "The bottom is so muddy; you would sink to your knees if you stepped in it. There's a city swimming pool in Eastville," she added helpfully, "but it's thirty miles away."

"I used to live right next to a lake," I reported as my shoulders slumped. With a weary sigh, I swung my bicycle around. "It's too hot to ride," I muttered. "I'm going home to set up my aquarium."

That afternoon, I was crouched behind a stack of unpacked boxes in our garage, hunting for my aquarium tank, when Alicia passed by with her mother. I heard her mom suggest that Alicia invite me to the rodeo coming to town next week.

"Devon won't want to go," Alicia immediately replied. "He's too busy missing his old home."

As Alicia's voice trailed off, I plopped down on the floor and seriously thought about her comment. Slowly, I realized the truth in her words. I had allowed my old memories to surround me like an invisible wall that blocked any positive view of my new home. I bit my lip as I gazed at a half-open box that held my old swimming tubes. Suddenly, I had an idea, and my feet felt light as I sprinted into the house.

Fifteen minutes later, Alicia and I were standing at the edge of the stock dam, while my dad supervised our adventure. We each had a swimming tube around our middle as we stepped into the water. Instantly, my foot sank into the mucky sponge, but I jumped in, letting the tube hold me above the muddy bottom.

After a moment's hesitation, Alicia timidly floated towards me, clinging tightly to her tube.

"I don't swim well," Alicia admitted, "but this water does feel amazing."

"Why don't I trade you swimming lessons for riding lessons?" I blurted. "I've seen you galloping through the pastures on your horse."

"Are you sure you want to learn to ride?" Alicia asked, surprised by my unexpected request.

"Yes!" I answered, and a glimmer of excitement bubbled up as I thought about climbing onto a saddle. At last, I was ready to dive into my new world with a tremendous splash.

GO ON →

8 The following question has two parts. First, answer part A. Then, answer part B.

Part A: Read the sentence from the text.

The sun watched us, blazing in the sky, its <u>punishing rays</u> beating down on our backs.

What does "punishing rays" mean?

(A) The sun feels just right.

(B) The sun is harming Devon.

(C) The sun feels very hot.

(D) The sun is following Devon.

Part B: Which phrase from the text supports your answer in part A?

(A) "silently pedaling"

(B) "gravel road"

(C) "watched us"

(D) "sweaty forehead"

GO ON →

9 Read the paragraph from the text.

"I wish we had a shady, wooded trail to ride on. There's nothing, not a tree or even a bush for miles," I grumbled, gazing at the <u>desolate</u> landscape, with nothing to see for miles. Suddenly, I noticed a sparkling blue pond nestled between some gentle hills. "Can we swim in that water?" I asked eagerly.

Which details from the paragraph help the reader understand what <u>desolate</u> means? Select **two** options.

(A) "shady"

(B) "nothing to see for miles"

(C) "wooded trail"

(D) "sparkling blue pond"

(E) "not a tree or even a bush"

(F) "gentle hills"

10 Check the boxes to indicate which detail describes each setting in the text.

Detail	Cattle Ranch	Lake Home
dusty air	☐	☐
the smell of pine trees	☐	☐
lack of trees	☐	☐
wooden cabin	☐	☐
pebbled beach	☐	☐
fresh breezes	☐	☐

GO ON →

11 How do Devon's feelings about his new home influence how the story is told in the beginning? Use **two** examples from the text to support your answer.

_____

_____

_____

_____

_____

_____

12 The following question has two parts. First, answer part A. Then, answer part B.

Part A: Which event in the text creates a change in Devon's attitude about his new home?

(A) pedaling up a gravel road to the top of a hill

(B) learning about a swimming pool in a nearby city

(C) being invited by Alicia to join her in a bicycle ride

(D) overhearing Alicia talking about him while in the garage

Part B: Which sentence from the text **best** supports your answer in part A?

(A) "Last spring, I had won first place in the crawl stroke contest at our club meet."

(B) "Slowly, I realized the truth in her words."

(C) "I stopped to rest, mopping my sweaty forehead with my hand."

(D) "Alicia was standing by the doorway, and she greeted me with an enthusiastic smile."

GO ON →

13 At the end of the text, how does Devon become more like Alicia? Select **all** that apply.

(A) He begins telling more jokes.

(B) He decides to make a new friend.

(C) He prefers the ranch over the lake.

(D) He wishes he were somewhere else.

(E) He tries to be happy with his surroundings.

(F) He wants to teach someone something new.

14 Read the sentence from the text.

"Yes!" I answered, and a glimmer of excitement <u>bubbled up</u> as I thought about climbing onto a saddle.

What does the idiom "bubbled up" mean?

(A) covered over

(B) lifted in the air

(C) appeared suddenly

(D) ended slowly

GO ON →

Read the texts. Then answer the questions.

A Spelunking Trip

The students in Ms. Odom's class arrived at Jarrett Cave on Saturday morning. It was not surprising that they had all shown up early, since they knew they were in for a real treat. They were going to become *spelunkers*. For weeks they had been studying about the wonderful world inside caves and how people called spelunkers explore them, mainly for fun or as a hobby. At last, the students were going to have a chance to become spelunkers too.

Ms. Odom and her assistant, Jason Jaramillo, were checking the equipment outside the cave while the class congregated around the entrance, anxious to see what was awaiting them. Two of the students, Karen and Binh, started to duck into the cave, but Ms. Odom stopped them. "Hey, you two, what are the first two rules of spelunking safety that we went over several times in class?"

Karen and Binh looked at the ground as Binh spoke, "We're sorry, Ms. Odom," Binh said. "The first rule is to always stay with an adult, and the second rule is not to leave the group."

GO ON →

Ms. Odom nodded and then smiled. "I'm sure it's hard to remember rules when you're excited about doing something for the first time, but the rules protect you from harm so you aren't vulnerable to it."

Before entering the cave, all of the students began to record their field notes. Ms. Odom said, "Include information about the air temperature outside the cave and about features near the cave's entrance. Inside, we will want to learn as much as possible about the cave's ecology." Shana looked at the thermometer posted at the entrance and quickly and accurately recorded the temperature, while Miguel took notes about the stream flowing from the cave.

Finally, the moment arrived, and the students prepared to go inside the cave. They all made sure they had their safety equipment. Everyone had to use helmets for protection, and the students also were given flashlights. They hastened into the cave and stood still until their eyes grew accustomed to the dim light. Jason told the class that they were in the "twilight zone" of the cave, and Ms. Odom explained why algae was growing on the top side of the rocks.

Everywhere the students looked, they saw something fascinating. Marcie discovered a brown-and-yellow cave cricket that she showed to the other students. Using their flashlights, everyone took notes about the variety of interesting things that surrounded them.

Next, they moved into the "dark zone" of the cave, where the students found an eerie world that was like nothing they had ever seen before. There was no natural light, and bats hung from the ceiling; the crickets were as pale as ghosts and had longer legs and antennae than the cricket Marcie had found earlier. Two students spotted some white, eyeless crayfish in the darkness, and Marcie noticed that these creatures didn't run away from the flashlight beams.

The spelunkers moved deeper into the cave, looking forward to each new discovery. This really was a trip to remember.

GO ON →

Exploring Mammoth Cave

Visitors enter the caves at Mammoth Cave National Park in Kentucky through a well-lit walkway. About 390 miles of connecting passages have been explored there, and scientists estimate there may be 600 more miles to go!

Three Young Explorers

In 1838, Franklin Gorin bought the property containing the cave mouth. He worked to build a hotel near the entrance and turned over the exploration of the cave to three enslaved African teenagers named Stephen Bishop, Mat Bransford, and Nick Bransford. A doctor named John Croghan bought the land and took ownership of the the youths the next year. At one time, Croghan treated patients at a special hospital inside the cave.

The three young men explored the cave with only candles and lanterns for light. They were the first to explore many miles of caves. They gave a name to each new wonder they found. They named passageways, such as Grand Avenue, and rock formations, such as a giant stone column called The Devil's Armchair. A large, open room was named The Church.

When they explored a new area, they often carved their names into a rocky wall. Sometimes they wrote their names on the ceiling using smoke from a candle, and many of these marks still survive. They show that the young men's outlook was similar to that of some modern cave explorers. They were willing to take great risks to discover what others had never seen.

Cave Tours

These young men gave day-long tours to people from all over the world. By exploring and talking with visitors who knew about caves, they became familiar with the geology of the cave. They knew how the cave was formed, and they learned the different types of rocks.

On some tours, visitors had to crawl on their hands and knees through a passage for more than 20 feet. Other tours included a boat ride down an underground river. Tourists had to lie down flat in the boat to pass beneath a low ceiling. The guides delighted in giving visitors a chance to "try the dark," which meant leaving the visitors for a few minutes in the pitch black of the caverns. Soon afterward, they led the visitors to the Star Chamber. When they looked up at the ceiling, it seemed that stars were glittering in a night sky.

GO ON →

The young men showed visitors the strange fish and shrimp living in the cave's waters. Some were completely white, and most had no eyes. They did not need eyes since there was never any light to help them see. The guides sometimes sold these fish to tourists to earn money.

U.S. National Park Service

Both Nick and Mat stayed near the natural wonder they had explored. They gave tours for many years. The next generations of Bransfords, as well as many other African Americans, gave tours until the 1930s when the U.S. National Park Service took over. The Mammoth Cave National Park officially opened in 1941. Then, in 2006, a fifth-generation member of the Bransford family began to give tours through the caverns. He was following in the footsteps of his ancestors.

Today, the U.S. National Park Service offers many different tours. Some of the tours follow the same routes that Stephen Bishop and the Bransfords took in the 1800s.

Popular Mammoth Cave Tours					
Name	**Highlights**	**Distance**	**Time**	**Elevation Change**	**Difficulty**
Grand Avenue	Snowball Room, Thorpe's Pit, Frozen Niagara	4 miles	$4\frac{1}{2}$ hr	280 ft	Strenuous
Historic	Historic entrance, Bottomless Pit, Mammoth Dome	2 miles	2 hr	300 ft	Moderate
Mammoth Passage	Largest rooms, early mining operations	$\frac{3}{4}$ mile	$1\frac{1}{4}$ hr	160 ft	Easy
River Styx	Underground rivers and Lake Lethe	$2\frac{1}{2}$ miles	$2\frac{1}{2}$ hr	360 ft	Moderate
Star Chamber	Star Chamber, John Croghan's hospital	$1\frac{1}{2}$ miles	$2\frac{1}{2}$ hr	160 ft	Moderate
Wild Cave	Crawling through caves with headlamps	5 miles	6 hr	300 ft	Very Difficult

GO ON →

Name: _____ Date: _____

Answer these questions about "A Spelunking Trip."

15 Read the sentence from the text.

Ms. Odom and her assistant, Jason Jaramillo, were checking the equipment outside the cave while the class <u>congregated</u> around the entrance, anxious to see what was awaiting them.

The root of <u>congregated</u> is a Latin word meaning "to flock together." What is the **most likely** meaning of <u>congregated</u>?

(A) gathered

(B) laughed and shouted

(C) pushed

(D) raced around quickly

16 Check the box to indicate the details from the text that describe the students in Ms. Odom's class and spelunkers. Some details describe **both**.

	students in Ms. Odom's class	spelunkers
required to follow the rules	☐	☐
required to learn new information about caves	☐	☐
explore caves as a hobby	☐	☐
enjoy exploring dark caves	☐	☐

GO ON →

17 "A Spelunking Trip" takes place in three different settings. Describe the differences in the settings. Use details from the text to support your answer.

_____

_____

_____

_____

_____

_____

GO ON →

Answer these questions about "Exploring Mammoth Cave."

18 The following question has two parts. First, answer part A. Then, answer part B.

Part A: Read the sentences from the text.

The Mammoth Cave National Park officially opened in 1941. Then, in 2006, a fifth-generation member of the Bransford family began to give tours through the caverns. He was <u>following in the footsteps</u> of his ancestors.

What does "following in the footsteps" mean in the sentences above?

(A) using a map

(B) remaining close by

(C) starting over again

(D) doing the same thing

Part B: Which phrase from the sentences provides the **best** support for your answer in part A?

(A) "in 2006"

(B) "began to give tours"

(C) "officially opened in 1941"

(D) "Mammoth Cave"

GO ON →

19 According to the chart, which tour of Mammoth Cave is most difficult, and which is easiest? Use details from the chart to support your answer.

_____

_____

_____

_____

_____

_____

20 The author would **most likely** agree with which statement?

Ⓐ Mammoth Cave should not be a tourist destination.

Ⓑ The Star Chamber is the most beautiful spot in the cave.

Ⓒ Early guides were important to the cave's exploration.

Ⓓ Tourists would have learned more from educated guides.

GO ON →

Name: _____ Date: _____

Now answer this question about "A Spelunking Trip" and "Exploring Mammoth Cave."

21 The students from the spelunking trip and the guides from Mammoth Cave both explored caves for fresh discoveries. Compare and contrast their experiences and the conditions they faced. Use details from the texts to support your answer.

_____

_____

_____

_____

_____

_____

_____

_____

_____

_____

_____

_____

_____

GO ON →

The text needs revision. Read the text. Then answer the questions.

(1) I love going to visit my grandmother she lives in Charleston. (2) During our last visit, we went down to her basement where she keeps old pictures. (3) I found some other stuff that really surprised me. (4) It was almost like she had a museum in her basement!

(5) She doesn't always throw away old things when they get replaced. (6) One of the old things was a phone with a dial. (7) Every hole in the dial had a number and letters like on phone buttons now. (8) You had to stick your finger in the hole, and then you turned it around to dial a number. (9) I tried dialing a number, and it took most time than using buttons!

(10) I found a "boom box," too. (11) It was one of the first music players you could carry with you. (12) But it was worser than music players today. (13) It was as big as a suitcase, and it felt even heavier. (14) Grandma said that people bought the most big ones in the store so they could play their music louder.

(15) I'm glad I've got my modern cell phone and a small music player. (16) They are more good than the old machines. (17) With these devices, I don't have to dial numbers or carry a big suitcase around to hear my music.

GO ON →

22 How can sentence 1 **best** be written?

(A) I love going to visit my grandmother, she lives in Charleston.

(B) I love going to visit my grandmother, lives in Charleston.

(C) I love going to visit my grandmother who lives in Charleston.

(D) I love going to visit my grandmother in Charleston, she lives there.

23 Which word in sentence 2 is an adjective that modifies a noun?

(A) During

(B) visit

(C) down

(D) old

24 Which sentence uses a relative adverb to introduce a subordinate clause?

(A) Sentence 2

(B) Sentence 4

(C) Sentence 7

(D) Sentence 15

25 Which sentence has two independent clauses?

(A) Sentence 5

(B) Sentence 6

(C) Sentence 7

(D) Sentence 8

GO ON →

26 Which sentence contains a dependent clause?

(A) Sentence 4

(B) Sentence 5

(C) Sentence 6

(D) Sentence 7

27 How can sentence 9 **best** be written?

(A) I tried dialing a number, and it took the most time than using buttons!

(B) I tried dialing a number, and it took greatest time than using buttons!

(C) I tried dialing a number, and it took morer time than using buttons!

(D) I tried dialing a number, and it took more time than using buttons!

28 How can sentence 12 be written correctly?

(A) But it was worst than music players today.

(B) But it was more worse than music players today.

(C) But it was worse than music players today.

(D) But it was baddest than music players today.

GO ON →

29 How can sentence 14 be written correctly?

Ⓐ Grandma said that people bought the more bigger ones in the store so they could play their music louder.

Ⓑ Grandma said that people bought the biggest ones in the store so they could play their music louder.

Ⓒ Grandma said that people bought the most bigger ones in the store so they could play their music louder.

Ⓓ Grandma said that people bought the most biggest ones in the store so they could play their music louder.

30 How can sentence 16 **best** be written?

Ⓐ They are better than the old machines.

Ⓑ They are gooder than the old machines.

Ⓒ They are more gooder than the old machines.

Ⓓ They are most good than the old machines.

31 Which word in sentence 17 is an adjective?

Ⓐ with

Ⓑ these

Ⓒ don't

Ⓓ around

STOP

Informational Performance Task

Task:

Your science class has been learning about how one small change in an environment can disrupt the balance of nature. Your teacher has asked everyone in the class to look up information about plants and animals introduced, purposely or by accident, to the United States, and their effect on the environment.

For this task, you will be writing an informational article related to the topic of invasive plants and animals. Before you write your article, you will review three sources that provide information about the topic.

After you have reviewed these sources, you will answer some questions about them. Briefly scan the sources and the three questions that follow. Then, go back and read the sources carefully to gain the information you will need to answer the questions and write an article.

In Part 2, you will write an informational article on a topic related to the sources.

Directions for Part 1

You will now read several sources. You can re-examine any of the sources as often as you like.

Research Questions:

After examining the sources, use the remaining time in Part 1 to answer three questions about them. Your answers to these questions will be scored. Also, your answers will help you think about the research sources you have read, which should help you write your informational article.

You may refer to the sources when you think it would be helpful. You may also refer to your notes.

GO ON →

Source #1: The New King of the River

In the 1970s, some Southern catfish farmers brought a newcomer, the Asian carp, to the United States. The farmers intended to use the carp to eat unwanted plants crowding their ponds. At first, their plan worked well. The carp feasted on the tiny, microscopic plants called algae and controlled their growth.

However, in time, a period of flooding occurred in the South, and the farmers' private ponds overflowed. Unfortunately, Asian carp escaped into nearby steams. Before long, they made their way into the Mississippi River.

An Ideal Environment

The Mississippi River offered the carp a perfect home. The greedy fish found ample food and devoured algae as well as other aquatic plants. In addition, the friendly, slow moving river did not contain any threatening predators; no fish in North America was large enough to eat an adult carp.

Unchecked, the carp population thrived. A large female carp is capable of producing a million eggs each year, so their numbers exploded. The carp spread, traveling up the Mississippi River and into connecting waterways.

A Destructive Force

Today, the imported fish has continued to flourish, but its habits are destroying the balance of nature in different rivers. The carp digest their food very rapidly, so food passes quickly through their system. As a result, the fish constantly feeds and can consume up to 40 percent of its body weight in a day.

Other small fish living in the rivers depend on the same plants for their food source, but they cannot compete with the ravenous carp. Without enough food to eat, the population of small fish has dropped. In turn, animals like turtles and birds, which eat small fish, also have less food.

The carp's continuous feeding strips away plants growing near shorelines, too. These plants are a key part of the habitat. They slow the movement of the stream. Without them, the rushing water begins to wash away riverbanks.

GO ON →

Problems for People

Asian carp also cause some unusual problems for people. One type of Asian carp is nicknamed the "flying fish." Loud noises, such as rumbling boat engines, startle the fish, which often swim together. When they are frightened, dozens of them suddenly soar into the air, jumping as high as ten feet. While such displays sound entertaining, the heavy, large fish have leapt into unsuspecting boats and struck their passengers, causing injuries.

A Dangerous Possibility

Over time, the Asian Carp has become the dominant fish in various rivers. For instance, 90% of the fish in the Illinois River are carp. Currently, a canal connects the Illinois River to Lake Michigan. People are very concerned the carp will enter Lake Michigan through the canal and slowly travel to other, adjoining Great Lakes.

Taking Steps

To prevent the problem, scientists have installed some steel bands that stretch across the canal entry. They produce an electric current that drives the carp back. At the same time, ships can still travel through the useful canal.

However, many people believe the canal should have a solid barrier. The Army Corps of Engineers has proposed building a series of fences. It would take 25 years to construct them. Other attempted control measures include netting carp and encouraging fishing.

Regrettably, the Asian carp is now a permanent resident in North America. Hopefully, with careful measures, people can limit its range. The future of a healthy Great Lakes habitat depends on it.

GO ON →

Source #2: A Super Bird

People know exactly how European starlings arrived in North America. One man, Eugene Schieffelin, is responsible for introducing the bird. The businessman had a peculiar scheme; he wanted to bring all the birds described in William Shakespeare's writings to our country. Some of the birds he imported, such as skylarks, disappeared and died.

However, the immigrant starling fared well. In 1891, Schieffelin released 80 of these birds in Central Park in New York City. A year later, excited birdwatchers discovered the first nesting pair of starlings across the street from the park in the eaves of a museum. In the years to come, the starlings spread much further than people ever imagined possible. They reached the west coast of California, traveled north to Alaska, and journeyed south to Florida.

Built for Success

How did the starling manage to swiftly adapt and prosper? The bird's physical characteristics provide it with certain advantages. First, the sturdy starling has more muscle than other similar-sized birds. As a result, it easily chases native birds from their prized homes, often stealing nests from bluebirds and woodpeckers.

The starling also has a sharp, strong bill. It can close its beak with enough force to crush its food. In addition, the starling can open its beak with surprising power. Using this trick, the starling creates gashes in the earth and aptly digs for insects, seeds, and other hidden fare.

Finally, the starling has excellent eyesight. Its eyes angle forward more than other birds' eyes do, giving the starling better frontal vision. The starling's eyes also have an unusual ability. One part of its eye can clearly see nearby objects, while another part of the eye is focusing on distant things. Because of this, starlings can effectively hunt for food and watch for danger at the same time.

Flocks of Problems

The starling's abilities have made it very successful at surviving. Often, the hearty birds raise two or three families a year. In the spring and fall, the social birds gather in large flocks, which may number in the thousands.

The vast groups of starlings cause a range of serious problems. At times, starlings descend on farmers' fields; the birds devour growing wheat and steal grain from cattle's troughs. They gobble orchards of cherries, vineyards of grapes, and tons of potatoes. Each year, starlings eat crops that are worth about 800 million dollars.

GO ON →

On occasion, enormous flocks of starlings take over town parks or choose roosting areas near homes or on city buildings. Their droppings soil the walkways and areas below them. Besides being dirty, the droppings carry diseases and present health hazards.

A Losing Battle

Chasing off flocks of starlings is extremely difficult. Many different methods have failed, such as frightening them with balloons, broadcasting threatening sounds, or spraying them with water. In the past, people have even tried putting electric wires or itching powder on buildings to discourage the nuisance birds from roosting. Sometimes, trained wildlife workers must trap and remove the unwanted birds.

Today, scientists estimate that 200 million starlings live in North America. Unfortunately, Schieffelin's eighty original birds are now one of the most abundant species in our country.

GO ON →

Source #3: Invasive Plants and Animals

The following information is part of a presentation on preventing the spread of invasive plants and animals.

Invasive Plants and Animals
How People Can Prevent and Help Stop Their Spread

Invasive Plants and Animals

They are plants and animals that are not native to the environment.

They damage habitats by:

- replacing native animals and plants
- upsetting food webs
- decreasing the water quality of streams and lakes
- introducing new diseases

A common plant invader called Kudzu.

Exactostock/Exactostock/SuperStock

GO ON →

How do invasive plants and animals arrive in North America?

Foreign plants and animals enter our country many ways.

- Some were brought to control animal or plant pests.

- Some were brought as pets.

- Some were accidently brought on ships.

- Some were accidently brought on imported plants and goods.

Once these invaders take hold, they are diffiucult to eliminate. Their numbers can explode. Today, about 4,300 invasive species live in North America.

Taking Important Steps

People can play a key role in limiting this serious problem.

- Do not release imported or exotic pets into the wild or take pets into protected wildlife areas.

- Never transport firewood from one region to another. The wood can be home to unwanted insects.

- In gardens, avoid growing non-native plants that produce lots of seeds that can spread to other areas.

- Do not bring home plants or animals from your vacation site when you travel.

- Volunteer with local park services and help remove invading plants in parks and recreational areas.

GO ON →

Name: _____ Date: _____

1 Draw a line between the Source #1 main idea and the detail from Source #3 that supports it.

Source #1 Main Idea	Source #3 Detail
Once introduced to an environment, non-native wildlife can rapidly reproduce.	"Once these invaders take hold, they are difficult to eliminate."
Removing non-native wildlife can be a challenging task.	"People can play a key role in limiting this serious problem."
Citizens must work together to prevent the spread of non-native plants.	"Their numbers can explode."

2 Source #1 and Source #2 both describe new ideas that were meant to create a positive change. Explain how each idea created a change in an unexpected way.

_____

_____

_____

_____

_____

_____

GO ON →

3 Explain why it is important to stop the spread of invasive plants and animals. Use at least **one** example from **each** source to support your explanation. For each example, include the source title or number.

_____

_____

_____

_____

_____

GO ON →

Directions for Part 2

You will now review your notes and sources, and plan, draft, revise, and edit your article. You may use your notes as reference to the sources. Now, read your assignment and the information about how your informational article will be scored; then begin your work.

Your Assignment:

Your class is studying invasive plants and animals. Your teacher has asked you to write a multi-paragraph article explaining how bringing foreign plants or animals into an environment may affect all living things. The audience for your article will be your classmates, and your teacher. In your article, clearly state your main idea and support your main idea with details using information from what you have read.

Now you are going to write your article to submit to your teacher. Choose the most important information from all three sources to support your ideas. Then, write an informational article that is several paragraphs long. Clearly organize your article and support your ideas with details from the sources. Use your own words except when quoting directly from the sources. Be sure to give the source title or number when including details from the sources.

REMEMBER: A well-written informational article

- has a clear main idea
- is well-organized and stays on the topic
- has an introduction and a conclusion
- uses transitions
- uses details from the sources to support your main idea
- develops ideas clearly
- uses clear language
- follows rules of writing (spelling, punctuation, and grammar)

Now begin work on your informational article. Manage your time carefully so that you can plan, write, revise, and edit the final draft of your informational article. Write your response on a separate sheet of paper.

Answer Key

Name: _____

Question	Correct Answer	Content Focus	CCSS	Complexity
1A	C	Context Clues: Paragraph Clues	L.5.4a	DOK 3
1B	C	Context Clues: Paragraph Clues/Text Evidence	L.5.4a/ RI.5.1	DOK 2
2	B, D	Greek Roots	L.5.4b	DOK 2
3	C	Context Clues: Paragraph Clues	L.5.4a	DOK 2
4	see below	Text Structure: Cause and Effect	RI.5.3	DOK 3
5A	A	Text Structure: Cause and Effect	RI.5.3	DOK 2
5B	B	Text Structure: Cause and Effect/Text Evidence	RI.5.3/ RI.5.1	DOK 2
6	C, F	Author's Point of View	RI.6.6	DOK 3
7A	A	Text Structure: Cause and Effect	RI.5.3	DOK 2
7B	C	Text Structure: Cause and Effect/Text Evidence	RI.5.3/ RI.5.1	DOK 2
8A	C	Literary Elements: Figurative Language	L.5.5c	DOK 2
8B	D	Literary Elements: Figurative Language/Text Evidence	L.5.5c/ RL.5.1	DOK 2
9	B, E	Context Clues: Paragraph Clues	L.5.4a	DOK 3
10	see below	Character, Setting, Plot: Compare and Contrast Settings	RL.5.3	DOK 2
11	see below	Literary Elements: Narrator	RL.5.6	DOK 3
12A	D	Character, Setting, Plot: Compare and Contrast Characters	RL.5.3	DOK 2
12B	B	Character, Setting, Plot: Compare and Contrast Characters/Text Evidence	RL.5.3/ RL/5.1	DOK 2
13	B, E, F	Character, Setting Plot: Compare and Contrast Characters	RL.5.3	DOK 3
14	C	Idioms	L.5.5b	DOK 2
15	A	Root Words	L.5.4b	DOK 2
16	see below	Character, Setting, Plot: Compare and Contrast Settings	RL.5.3	DOK 2
17	see below	Character, Setting, Plot: Compare and Contrast Settings	RL.5.3	DOK 3
18A	D	Idioms	L.5.5b	DOK 2
18B	B	Idioms/Text Evidence	L.5.5b/ RI.5.1	DOK 2
19	see below	Text Features: Chart	RI.4.7	DOK 3
20	C	Author's Point of View	RI.6.6	DOK 3

Name: _____

Question	Correct Answer	Content Focus	CCSS	Complexity
21	see below	Compare Across Texts	W.5.9	DOK 4
22	C	Complex Sentences	L.5.1	DOK 1
23	D	Adjectives	L.5.1	DOK 1
24	A	Complex Sentences	L.5.1	DOK 1
25	D	Independent and Dependent Clauses	L.5.1	DOK 1
26	B	Independent and Dependent Clauses	L.5.1	DOK 1
27	D	Adjectives That Compare	L.5.1	DOK 1
28	C	Comparing with *Good* and *Bad*	L.5.1	DOK 1
29	B	Adjectives That Compare	L.5.1	DOK 1
30	A	Comparing with *Good* and *Bad*	L.5.1	DOK 1
31	B	Adjectives	L.5.1	DOK 1

Comprehension: Selected Responses 5A, 5B, 6, 7A, 7B, 12A, 12B, 13, 20	/12	%
Comprehension: Constructed Response 4, 10, 11, 16, 17, 19, 21	/16	%
Vocabulary 1A, 1B, 2, 3, 8A, 8B, 9, 14, 15, 18A, 18B	/16	%
English Language Conventions 22–31	/10	%
Total Unit Assessment Score	/54	%

4 **2-point response:** Doctors believed that the human body held four humors, and those humors had to be balanced. Blood was one of the humors. A person who got sick had too much "bad blood," so it had to be removed to heal the patient.

10 Students should choose the following for each detail:
- dusty air: Cattle Ranch
- the smell of pine trees: Lake Home
- lack of trees: Cattle Ranch
- wooden cabin: Cattle Ranch
- pebbled beach: Lake Home
- fresh breezes: Lake Home

11 **2-point response:** Devon is not happy because he misses his home by a "beautiful lake." He is sad, and his first-person descriptions show his sadness. The cows he sees are "black smudges," and the prairie is a "sea of lonely fields."

16 Students should choose the following for each detail:
- required to follow the rules: Students in Ms. Odom's class *and* Spelunkers
- required to learn new information about caves: Students in Ms. Odom's class
- explore caves as a hobby: Spelunkers
- enjoy exploring dark caves: Students in Ms. Odom's class *and* Spelunkers

17 **2-point response:** The story contains three different settings: outside the cave, the "twilight zone" of the cave, and the cave's "dark zone." The first setting is brighter than the two cave settings. The "twilight zone" has dim light, while the third setting is called "the dark zone" because there is no natural light at all. Here there are "eyeless crayfish" that have no need of vision.

19 **2-point response:** The Wild Cave tour is the most difficult. It lasts 6 hours, covers 5 miles, and involves crawling through caves. The Mammoth Passage tour is easiest. It lasts only 1¼ hours and goes ¾ mile through the largest rooms.

21 **4-point response:** The early explorers of Mammoth Cave had only simple equipment, such as candles and a ladder, while the class trip was prepared with flashlights, helmets, and scientific equipment, such as thermometers. The early explorers had to take many chances to explore new passages while the school trip was visiting an area well-known to the teachers. The early explorers loved the cave and became very knowledgeable about the geology. Exploring on the class trip would add to the students' scientific knowledge and might inspire them to learn more about caves or related scientific subjects.

Answer Key

Name: _____

Informational Performance Task					
Question	Answer	CCSS		Complexity	Score
1	see below	RI.5.1, RI.5.2, RI.5.7, RI.5.9 W.5.2a-e, W.5.4, W.5.7 L.5.1, L.5.2		DOK 2	/1
2	see below			DOK 3	/2
3	see below			DOK 3	/2
Informational Article	see below			DOK 4	/4 [P/O] /4 [E/E] /2 [C]
Total Score					**/15**

1 Students should match the following main ideas and details:
- **Source #1:** Once introduced to an environment, non-native wildlife can rapidly reproduce.
  Source #3: "Their numbers can explode and become established."
- **Source #1:** Removing non-native wildlife can be a challenging task.
  Source #3: "Once these invaders take hold, they are difficult to eliminate."
- **Source #1:** Citizens must work together to prevent the spread of non-native plants.
  Source #3: "People can play a key role in limiting this serious problem."

2 **2-point response:** In Source #1, farmers hoped to use the Asian carp to eat unwanted plants that crowded their ponds. Unfortunately, the carp made it out of the ponds and into larger waterways. Their appearance disrupted the balance of these rivers and lakes.

In Source #2, Eugen Schieffelin wanted to introduce all of the birds from William Shakespeare's writings into the United States. While many of the birds did not survive, the starling did. It quickly overpowered native birds, destroyed crops, and dirtied public areas.

3 **2-point response:** It is important to stop the spread of invasive plants and animals because once it starts, it is very hard to control or stop. Source #1 tells about the difficulties scientists have encountered blocking carp from Lake Michigan. Source #2 tells how the many efforts to control the starlings have failed. Source #3 tells how the numbers of invasive species can grow quickly and greatly.

10-point anchor paper: Living things have established habitats. There is an order to their lives so that their needs are met. When a new plant or animal is brought into the habitat, the food web is changed. This means that some animals or plants will become food for the new living thing. The population of some animals or plants will decrease.

Sometimes people bring animals to the US to control or rid an area of living things that are not wanted. This is the case of the Asian carp that were brought to eat algae from the lakes and ponds where catfish are raised. The farmers who brought them had not considered what would happen if the fish were introduced into other bodies of water. When that did happen, the population of carp increased and the population of small fish decreased. The food web was changed, and some animal and plant populations decreased.

People who desire to have exotic animals as pets must consider what could happen if the animals escaped from their controlled habitat. These animals could upset the balance of life in many different habitats. The result could be the loss of animals and plants that are used as food for other living things. People need to be informed about the effects these animals could have on all living things in the environment.

Answer Key

Name: _____

Sometimes new plants or animals are introduced into a habitat by accident. This may happen when people move seeds from one place to another. It can also happen by moving firewood.

Sometimes new plants and animals are introduced into a habit with good intentions. This is what happened with the starling. However, adding this bird did more than bring a Shakespeare bird to North America. The introduction of the starling became a nuisance to other birds and to the local populations it inhabited.

There are currently about 4,300 invasive species living in North America. Once they are here, it is difficult to get rid of these living things. We can, however, prevent adding to the list of invaders by being careful with what we bring into our environment.

Read the text. Then answer the questions.

A Letter to the Editor

To the editor of *Oliver Community News:*

I would like readers of this newspaper to know about a special community event. It is the yearly art show of Oliver High School's Pen and Ink Club. At this special event, attendees will get to view works of up-and-coming young artists in our community. Each drawing at the art show has been carefully created in one of the most demanding and unforgiving mediums of the art world.

Most people haven't heard the phrase "pen and ink drawing." However, they have probably seen at least one such drawing in their lifetime, perhaps an illustration in a book or a framed piece of artwork hanging on the wall. Many talented artists have used this medium, from Michelangelo to Picasso. Many book illustrators use pen and ink drawings as well.

Pen and ink drawing is much like a pencil drawing, yet it is a little trickier to learn. The most difficult part of learning it is the fact that the ink is permanent. The artist cannot make a mistake because the ink cannot be erased.

Here are some details about the upcoming show. It is titled "Creatures in Ink." The opening is on Friday, November 2, at 6:30 P.M., in the Oliver Community Center next door to the high school. The drawings will remain on exhibit for three weeks after the opening.

In my opinion, "Creatures in Ink" is the best art show our club has ever held. Everyone who has already seen the drawings agrees with this opinion. These drawings leap off the paper and grab you by the collar.

Many people have said that there are even more talented students taking part in the club this year than usual. The proof of that talent is the many beautiful and lifelike drawings in the show. A reporter for our school newspaper interviewed our principal about the Pen and Ink Club and the upcoming show. She told the reporter that she was proud to be part of a school with such gifted students.

Finally, Javier Ramos, a famous artist who once attended Oliver High, came to see the drawings as they were being prepared for the show. He commented that the work was incredible. He said that when he was in high school, his drawings were not nearly as good, In fact, he said that his drawing skills at that time were rudimentary compared to what he saw here.

GO ON →

In the show, you'll see ink drawings of creatures such as dinosaurs, birds, lizards, spiders, and monkeys. The artists studied photographs or other pictures of the creatures they chose to draw. They studied the creature's muscles and imagined how it would move in the wild. Then they created drawings showing the creatures in their natural habitats. Each drawing took weeks, maybe months, to create, and all of the drawings look very realistic when completed. Some scenes are so thoroughly drawn that it takes special attention to locate a shy creature in its home environment. This art show will require you to use your skills as a careful observer. It is necessary to spend time in front of each drawing in order to appreciate the many details.

Several people who have seen the drawings have said that the Pen and Ink Club should be given a special prize for the quality of work its members have produced. I'm confident that by the time the exhibit is over, the entire community will love "Creatures in Ink." No one will leave the show disappointed.

Andrew Warrel

Secretary, Pen and Ink Club

Pen and ink drawing is not for everyone, but artists who choose to work with ink say that it is worth all the trouble. They like it because they can create pictures that are very exact.

GO ON →

1 Which details support the idea that pen and ink drawing is more difficult than other types of drawing? Select **two** options.

(A) The drawings may include hidden creatures.

(B) Most people have not heard of it.

(C) The drawings cannot be erased.

(D) Famous artists have used this medium.

(E) Artists must carefully plan to avoid making mistakes.

(F) Examples can be found in art books.

2 Read the sentence from the text.

These drawings leap off the paper and grab you by the collar.

What does this sentence mean?

(A) The drawings are difficult to hang on walls.

(B) These drawings jump on your shirt and hold onto your collar.

(C) The drawings leave ink stains on your collar if you grab them.

(D) These drawings are so good that they really get your attention.

GO ON →

3 Why does the writer directly tell the reader "to use your skills as a careful observer" when they go to the show? Select **two** choices.

Ⓐ to warn that it might be difficult to understand the drawings

Ⓑ to tell that the drawings will be judged for a prize

Ⓒ to create excitement about the artwork on display

Ⓓ to explain how pen and pencil drawings are different

Ⓔ to challenge them to look for mistakes in the drawings

Ⓕ to encourage them to attend the show

4 Read the paragraph from the text.

Finally, Javier Ramos, a famous artist who once attended Oliver High, came to see the drawings as they were being prepared for the show. He commented that the work was incredible. He said that when he was in high school, his drawings were not nearly as good. In fact, he said that his drawing skills at that time were rudimentary compared to what he saw here.

Select the phrase that helps you understand what rudimentary means in the paragraph above.

Ⓐ "a famous artist"

Ⓑ "work was incredible"

Ⓒ "not nearly as good"

Ⓓ "drawing skills"

GO ON →

Name: _____ **Date:** _____

5 Read the sentence from the text.

Each drawing took weeks, maybe months, to <u>create</u>, and all the drawings look very realistic when completed.

Which word has the **opposite** meaning of the word <u>create</u>?

(A) appreciate

(B) destroy

(C) spend

(D) invent

6 Why did the artists study their subjects so closely?

(A) so their art would be as real as possible

(B) because they had an entire school year to complete the art

(C) because they wanted to impress the artist Javier Ramos

(D) so their art show would become a big hit

(E) He commented that the work was incredible.

(F) You'll see ink drawings of dinosaurs, birds, lizards, spiders, and monkeys

GO ON →

7 The author included a sample of artwork in the text. Which idea in the text does the illustration support? Use details from the text in your response.

_____

_____

_____

_____

_____

Read the text. Then answer the questions.

The Choice

Two more weeks was all that stood between Jesse and his tenth birthday! He felt taller just thinking about it. Being double digits was a big deal, and so was the epic birthday party Jesse was hoping to have with all of his friends. Stronger, popular, excited, older.

The party was such a big deal that Jesse had been in his bedroom for an eternity debating who he should invite. Should it be a massive party with everyone he knew, or should he keep it small so that he could spend more time with each of his closest friends?

It was not long before Jesse was summoned by his mom. "Do you have that list for me yet, Jesse?" she called up the stairs. He hurriedly wrote down the final name —Tim, a friend he had been playing soccer with for two years. Then, clutching the list like a prized possession, he sprinted down the stairs, relieved to deliver the news to his mom. She scrutinized it, and Jesse could almost read her mind. "What's wrong, Mom?"

"Well," she began, "I see that you invited all of the boys in your class except Michael, the boy who just moved here from Indiana."

"I know," Jesse began to explain, getting defensive, "but I don't know him very well at all. He probably wouldn't like the activities we have planned and wouldn't have any fun."

His mom was quiet for a moment. "It's your party," she said, "but I want you to spend the next day giving that some additional consideration. In all probability, Michael doesn't know many people here yet, and he may appreciate being included. Also, what if he finds out that he was the only boy not invited?"

"Fine," Jesse said, heading back up to his room to play video games, not intending to give it much thought at all. But, later that day, he reluctantly found that he was not only thinking about his new classmate, Michael, but also about when he himself first started playing soccer.

GO ON →

That first day, he was anxious and hesitant to step out on the field. He wasn't exactly an introvert, but it did take him some time to get accustomed to new situations and make friends. Plus, he knew that most of the team had been playing longer, and they had already developed connections. Lucky for him, Tim was on his team. Even though no one was rude, it was Tim who made sure he was included in all of the goofing around that occurred after practice and always called him over to sit next to him when the team went out for food after a big win. Two years later, it was this same Tim he considered his closest friend.

So, when Jesse distributed the invitations at school the following day, his stack included one for Michael. As the class proceeded outside for recess, his teacher, Mrs. Marks, requested that Jesse remain behind for a minute. "Great," thought Jesse, "what did I do wrong now?" But Mrs. Marks wore a big smile when he approached.

"I noticed that you invited Michael to your party," she said.

"Yes," Jesse replied, feeling slightly unaccustomed to such positive attention from his teacher. He knew that Mrs. Marks felt that he needed to work harder from time to time.

"Well, I think that was a wonderful and gracious thing to do for someone who is new," she continued. "You probably don't realize this, but Michael's dad is still working in Indiana and will be there for a few more months. I know that's been difficult for Michael, and I'm sure this invitation will mean a lot to him and his mom."

Jesse had no idea about Michael's dad, or why his mom would care about a party, but Jesse felt good knowing that Mrs. Marks was proud of him. In fact, Michael's mom was the first to call and accept the invitation to the party. She said that Michael was really looking forward to it.

When the day of the party came, Jesse felt like he was going to explode with excitement. Tim was the first to arrive, and he and Jesse started playing basketball in the driveway. Michael came next, and he stood off to the side watching them. Looking at Tim, and then Michael, Jesse remembered that first season of soccer. He tossed the ball to Michael, who surprised them by making a nearly impossible shot from where he was standing! "Whoa! How did you do that?" Jesse exclaimed. From then on the party flew by. By the time everyone went home, Jesse was thankful that he had been given the push he needed to find a new friendship.

GO ON →

Name: _____ Date: _____

8 The following question has two parts. First, answer part A. Then, answer part B.

Part A: Who is the narrator of the text?

Ⓐ Jesse

Ⓑ an outside observer

Ⓒ Jesse's mom

Ⓓ a minor character

Part B: Which sentence from the text **best** shows the influence of the narrator's point of view?

Ⓐ "'Do you have that list for me yet, Jesse?' she called up the stairs."

Ⓑ Michael came next, and he stood off to the side watching them.

Ⓒ "'He probably wouldn't like the activities we have planned and wouldn't have any fun.'"

Ⓓ That first day, he was anxious and hesitant to step out on the field.

9 Read the paragraph from the text.

The party was such a big deal that Jesse had been in his bedroom for an eternity debating who he should invite. Should it be a massive party with everyone he knew, or should he keep it small so that he could spend more time with each of his closest friends?

Draw a line between the word from the text and the correct definition of the word.

careful

a long time

eternity   larger than usual

massive   punishment

a moment

very expensive

10 Read the sentence from the text.

Then, clutching the list like a prized possession, he sprinted down the stairs, relieved to deliver the news to his mom.

Which ideas do the descriptive details in this sentence support? Choose **two** options.

(A) Jesse is careless.

(B) Jesse is a skilled athlete.

(C) Jesse wants to please his mother.

(D) Jesse is happy about his decision.

(E) Jesse is excited about his birthday party.

(F) Jesse thinks about the feelings of others.

GO ON →

Name: _____ Date: _____

11 The following question has two parts. First, answer part A. Then, answer part B.

Part A: What main purpose does the flashback serve in the text?

(A) It reveals Jesse's reason for joining the soccer team.

(B) It shows how Jesse begins to understand Michael's situation.

(C) It tells why Jesse and Tim begin playing soccer together.

(D) It describes how Jesse and Tim help each other when necessary.

Part B: Which sentence from the text **best** supports your answer in part A?

(A) "But, later that day, he reluctantly found that he was not only thinking about his new classmate, Michael, but also about when he himself first started playing soccer. "

(B) "Plus, he knew that most of the team had been playing longer, and they had already developed connections."

(C) "Even though no one else was rude, it was Tim who made sure he was included in all of the goofing around that occurred after practice and always called him over to sit next to him when the team went out for food after a big win."

(D) "Two years later, it was this same Tim he considered his closest friend."

GO ON →

12 How does the narrator present Mrs. Marks?

Ⓐ as a nosy character

Ⓑ as a confused character

Ⓒ as a mean character

Ⓓ as a caring character

13 The following question has two parts. First, answer part A. Then, answer part B.

Part A: What is the theme of the text?

Ⓐ Practice and patience pay off.

Ⓑ Respect your elders.

Ⓒ Showing kindness to others is always worthwhile.

Ⓓ Good friendships are strong from the very start.

Part B: Which detail from the text **best** supports your answer in part A?

Ⓐ "He hurriedly wrote down the final name—Tim, a friend he had been playing soccer with for two years."

Ⓑ "Two years later, it was this same Tim he considered his closest friend."

Ⓒ "In fact, Michael's mom was the first to call and accept the invitation to the party."

Ⓓ "He knew that Mrs. Marks felt that he needed to work harder from time to time."

GO ON →

14 Jesse decides to invite a new boy in school to his tenth birthday party. How does his decision support the theme of the text? Use **two** details from the text to support your response.

_____

_____

_____

_____

_____

_____

GO ON →

Read the texts. Then answer the questions.

Amelia Earhart: Pioneer

Amelia Earhart was born in 1897 in a small Kansas town. That was six years before the Wright brothers took their famous first airplane flight in Kitty Hawk, North Carolina. Over the next two decades, aviation developed rapidly, but the pilots at the controls were mainly men. Amelia Earhart broke through that barrier to become a famous aviator, and she paved the way for women who followed.

Amelia Takes Off

Amelia took her first flying lesson in 1921. At the end of the year, she received her pilot's license. She took odd jobs and received financial help from her mother to buy her own airplane. With a plane of her own, Amelia quickly began making a name for herself in the aviation world. In October 1922, she broke a world record for female pilots by flying her plane to 14,000 feet in altitude. In 1923, she received her International Pilot's License—just the sixteenth woman in the world to do so. Unfortunately, Amelia had to sell her plane to give her mother money, and for a while, her love of aviation became more of a hobby.

But this all changed in 1928 when Amelia was contacted by publisher George Putnam, who she later married. He invited her to be a passenger on a cross-Atlantic flight. Amelia would have preferred to be the pilot, not the passenger, but at the time, flying a plane over an ocean was considered too dangerous for women.

The flight was successful, and Amelia became world-famous as the first woman to fly across the Atlantic. However, Amelia was not satisfied. She did not get to operate the controls during the flight and thought of herself as being no more important to the flight's success than "a sack of potatoes." She was determined to fly on her own.

GO ON →

Amelia Reaches Stardom

In 1929, Amelia became involved with an organization called the Ninety-Nines, a group that promoted female pilots in the aviation industry. She was the group's first president. In May of 1932, Amelia crossed the Atlantic again, but this time she was at the controls. She made the trip from Canada to Ireland in 15 hours. She received many medals and awards for her achievement.

Amelia hoped her success would open doors for women in aviation and in other fields, so she continued flying and setting records. She became the first person to fly across both the Atlantic and Pacific oceans when she flew from Hawaii to California.

An Extraordinary Mission

Even after proving she was a world-class aviator, Amelia still wanted more. In 1937, she set off on an amazing trip: flying around the world. Amelia started in California but faced trouble along the way. She became ill, her plane needed repairs, and bad weather forced a change in the flight route. She made it to one of her planned stops near Australia, but she never made it to her next destination. People all over the world were following the news of Amelia's trip—and now she was missing! President Franklin D. Roosevelt conducted a $4 million rescue mission, but Amelia was never found.

Amelia hoped that her actions would inspire other women to follow their dreams. One of her lifelong missions was for the world to recognize that women could have the same careers as men. Even though she died at a young age, just 40 years old, Amelia was an inspiration to many.

GO ON →

A Basketball Dream

"How many points do you think you'll score today, Jason" my friend Max asks as I wrap my leg with an elastic bandage.

"I'm hoping to manage at least 20. You?" I reply as I finish wrapping. Then Max and I join the team at the end of the court.

My leg isn't wrapped because of an injury. I wrap it before every game to make sure I don't injure other people! This may sound strange, but let me explain; I was born without a tibia in my right leg (your tibia is the shin bone below your knee), and when I was just two years old, I got a prosthetic leg. It's made of metal and plastic, so I wrap it in case another player bumps into me. If you didn't know I had a prosthetic leg, you probably wouldn't be able to tell. At first, my parents and friends thought it would be too difficult for me to play basketball because of my leg, but they soon found out I can play just as well as anyone!

I began playing basketball when I was three, when my father placed a small plastic hoop on the back of my bedroom door. Every day, I took practice shots with an orange foam ball. When I got older, my parents installed a real hoop in our driveway. Every day after school, I could be found in my driveway, dribbling the ball and shooting hoops. My hard work paid off because I made the team as a sixth grader. I've never let my leg stop me from reaching my goals.

I remember the first time I stepped onto the basketball court to play in a game. My head was swimming with the sounds of cheering fans. I hadn't thought I'd be nervous, but I was, and I realized that this was going to be very different from playing in the driveway with my dad! When my teammate won the tip-off, the orange orb headed straight for me. I caught it but felt like I was frozen in place. I soon came back to reality, turned, and headed down the court, the sound of the bouncing ball echoing in my ears. From that moment on, my playing has improved; every game I get better and better, sprinting up and down the court, keeping up with the other players. The ball is like a streak of lightning as I pass it across the court, and the net seems to nod its head with approval after almost every shot I take.

I take my position on the court and get ready for the tip-off. I keep a close eye on number 45, just as Coach instructed earlier. I can tell he's a good player by the way he dribbles the ball effortlessly between his legs. Suddenly, he takes a shot, but I leap into the air and swat away the ball, blocking his shot! My teammate Tommy grabs the ball, runs down the court, and takes an easy shot to score the first points of the game. Now that's how to start a game!

GO ON →

Name: _____ Date: _____

Answer these questions about "Amelia Earhart: Pioneer."

15 Draw a line from the definition of the word to a homophone of that word.

way

route

ordinary; common

flew

to see how heavy something is

plane

sack

16 After her first cross-Atlantic flight, why did Amelia say that she was no more important than a "sack of potatoes"?

(A) She did not have the skills required to be a pilot.

(B) She did not get to operate the controls during the flight.

(C) She thought she had stopped the flight from being a success.

(D) She wanted to show that she was satisfied with the experience.

17 What problems did Amelia face once she decided she wanted to become a pilot, and how did she solve those problems? Use details from the text to support your answer.

_____

_____

_____

_____

_____

GO ON →

Answer these questions about "A Basketball Dream."

18 Read the sentence from the text.

The ball is like a streak of lightning as I pass it across the court, and <u>the net seems to nod its head with approval</u> after almost every shot I take.

Why does the author compare the net to a person nodding?"

(A) To show that the net seems very large.

(B) To show how the net flops because it is broken.

(C) To show how much more practice Jason needs.

(D) To show that Jason is playing well.

19 Which detail from the text **best** supports the idea that Jason has determination?

(A) "I wrap it before every game to make sure I don't injure other people!"

(B) "I keep a close eye on number 45, just as Coach instructed earlier."

(C) "I've never let my leg stop me from reaching my goals."

(D) "I caught it but felt like I was frozen in place."

20 What effect does Jason's flashback about his first game have on the plot? Use details from the text to support your answer.

_____

_____

_____

_____

_____

GO ON →

Name: _____ Date: _____

Now answer this question about "Amelia Earhart: Pioneer" and "A Basketball Dream."

21 In "Amelia Earhart: Pioneer" and "A Basketball Dream," Amelia and Jason both do things that others do not think they can do. Explain how their experiences teach others about achieving their goals. Use details from both texts to support your answer.

_____

_____

_____

_____

_____

_____

_____

_____

_____

_____

_____

_____

_____

GO ON →

The text below needs revision. Read the text. Then answer the questions.

(1) Elizabeth sat in the kitchen and washed her father's soiled shirt. (2) She rubbed it against the washboard back and forth that was set in the basin. (3) The water quickly turned brown as Elizabeth washed the mud away. (4) Suddenly, Elizabeth heard her parents' voices in the next room. (5) She stopped rubbing the shirt and listened closer.

(6) "William, I'm going to the sit-in tomorrow," said her mother. (7) "Women should have a right to vote in this town."

(8) "Victoria, of course I agree with you," her father said. (9) "But I'm worried that the protesters will be arrested!"

(10) Elizabeth's mother answered firmly. (11) "I'm sorry, but you can't never change my mind. (12) I'm going to the town hall. (13) I will be there at 8 a.m. tomorrow."

(14) "I wish you didn't have to do this, but I understand your reasons," said Father.

(15) Elizabeth could hear him walking. (16) He was coming toward the kitchen.

GO ON →

22 How can sentence 2 **best** be written?

(A) Against the washboard that was set in the basin back and forth she rubbed it.

(B) Rubbed it against the washboard that was set in the basin back and forth she did.

(C) She rubbed it against the washboard that was set in the basin back and forth.

(D) She rubbed it back and forth against the washboard that was set in the basin.

23 How can sentence 5 be written correctly?

(A) She stopped rubbing the shirt and listened most close.

(B) She stopped rubbing the shirt and listened more close.

(C) She stopped rubbing the shirt and listened most closest.

(D) She stopped rubbing the shirt and listened more closely.

24 How can sentence 11 **best** be written?

(A) "I'm sorry, but you can't change my mind."

(B) "I'm sorry, but you can't not ever change my mind."

(C) "I'm sorry, but you cannot never change my mind."

(D) "I'm sorry, but you can't hardly change my mind."

GO ON →

25 How can sentences 12 and 13 **best** be combined?

(A) "I will be at the town hall at 8 A.M. tomorrow."

(B) "Tomorrow, I'm going to the town hall at 8 A.M., I will be there."

(C) "I'm going to the town hall, I will be there at 8 A.M. tomorrow."

(D) "Because I'm going to the town hall, I will be there at 8 A.M. tomorrow."

26 Which revision **best** combines sentences 15 and 16?

(A) Elizabeth could hear him toward the kitchen walking.

(B) Elizabeth could hear him walking toward the kitchen.

(C) Elizabeth could hear him walking and he was coming toward the kitchen.

(D) Elizabeth could hear him toward the kitchen coming and walking.

GO ON →

The text below needs revision. Read the text. Then answer the questions.

Elizabeth's father came ___(1)___ and poured himself a drink of water. Elizabeth didn't want to let him know she had been listening to his conversation, but she couldn't help herself. "Father, why ___(2)___ Mother be able to vote?" she asked.

He looked at her ___(3)___ for a moment and then pulled up a chair next to the washbasin. "Well, some men in the town think that men should be the only people allowed to vote. What do you think about that?"

Elizabeth sat up straight and crossed her arms. "I don't think that's right. Women should be treated ___(4)___ , and we should have the same rights as men," she stated.

"Unfortunately, not everyone thinks that way. But I have a feeling that your mother is going to change that ___(5)___ she gets to the town hall tomorrow," he said. Then his eyes lit up, and he smiled. "In fact, I think I'll go down there and sit with her."

GO ON →

27 Which answer should go in blank (1)?

Ⓐ the kitchen

Ⓑ into the kitchen

Ⓒ after the kitchen

28 Which answer should go in blank (2)?

Ⓐ shouldn't not

Ⓑ shouldn't never

Ⓒ shouldn't

29 Which answer should go in blank (3)?

Ⓐ thoughtful

Ⓑ thoughtfully

Ⓒ more thoughtful

30 Which answer should go in blank (4)?

Ⓐ more thoughtful

Ⓑ fairer

Ⓒ more fairly

31 Which answer should go in blank (5)?

Ⓐ when

Ⓑ so

Ⓒ although

STOP

Opinion Performance Task

Task:

Your class has been learning about ways people affect the environment. Now the mayor has proposed a plan to build a new highway near your town. As editor of the school newspaper, you have decided to write a multi-paragraph article to give an opinion about the mayor's proposal. Before you begin, you do some research and find two articles and a presentation about how the changes humans make can affect animals and plants living around them.

After you have reviewed these sources, you will answer some questions about them. Briefly scan the sources and the three questions that follow. Then, go back and review the sources carefully to gain the information you will need to answer the questions and finalize your research. You may take notes on the information you find in the sources as you read. Your notes will be available to you as you answer the questions

Directions for Part 1

You will now examine three sources. You can look at these sources as often as you like.

Research Questions:

After examining the sources, use the rest of the time in Part 1 to answer the three questions. Your answers to these questions will be scored. Also, your answers will help you think about the information you have read and viewed, which should help you write your article.

You may take notes when you think it would be helpful.

GO ON →

Source #1: An Invisible Pollution

Cities throb with sound. Airplanes thunder overhead, traffic rumbles by, and horns blare. As populations grow, these noise levels constantly increase. They are an invisible type of pollution that upsets the balance of nature.

Hearing, a Valuable Sense
Most animals have well-developed hearing. They depend on this sharp sense to avoid danger, and, sometimes, loud sounds interfere with their ability to escape predators.

For example, scientists studied how dune buggy noise affected the desert kangaroo rat. First, they exposed the rat to bursts of the noise. Then they tested how quickly the rat responded to the *swish* of an approaching snake. Usually, the rat kicks sand at this enemy when it is about 16 inches away. However, after listening to blasts of a dune buggy, the rat did not react until the snake crept within an inch. This is a severe disadvantage for the endangered rat.

For some animals, loud noises prevent their mating success. Certain animals rely on mating calls to attract partners, but noise masks their songs. This is especially true for several species of tree frogs, and scientists say the noise could eventually lead to decreases in frog populations.

Other animals, like the German nightingale, have attempted to overcome city noises by singing with more piercing melodies. Their songs now reach 95 decibels, the same volume as a roaring chainsaw. Certain birds have tried changing the pitch of their songs, too, or singing at night after daytime sounds fade. By adjusting their calls, the birds may be able to survive noisy challenges.

Changing Habits
Loud noises cause animals to modify other behaviors, too. Today, aircraft frequently fly over wildlife regions. Their constant rumbling can upset animals living beneath their flight patterns. As a result, some animals, like the endangered palila bird in Hawaii, leave prime nesting locations and crowd into peaceful, less-suitable areas.

In some cases, low-flying planes frighten herds of animals, causing stampedes. The frantic racing leads to injuries. This is a special concern when planes disrupt herds with young calves. One study tracked several caribou herds. The herd that experienced the most overhead flights lost the most calves.

GO ON →

Links in a Chain

When one animal alters its behavior, the change can ripple through the environment. Scientists unraveled a perfect example when they studied the relationship between hummingbirds, Western scrub jays, mice, and pinyon pine trees. The loud noise from natural gas wells sets off the chain of events.

To begin with, the clatter of the noisy wells chased jays from the surrounding areas; jays preferred quiet settings. Once the jays disappeared, hummingbirds quickly moved into the location. Because jays usually raid their nests, with the jays gone, the noisy sites now favored the hummingbirds. The hummingbirds fed on flowers, spread their pollen, and helped flowers grow.

However, the absence of jays hurt the pine trees. Often, jays eat the trees' seeds and stash extra seeds in the ground, encouraging seedlings to sprout.

After the jay disappeared, mice feasted on the available seeds. Unlike jays, mice left few seeds behind. In time, few seedlings were found near wells. The noisy sound had led to a decrease in the number of pine trees.

How loud is your world?

Today, scientists continue to investigate the impacts of noise pollution. Our government is also working to limit these problems through the Noise Control Act, which has lessened aircraft noise. You can help, too, by turning down the volume of things, like televisions, and by shutting off machines, like fans, when they are not being used.

Look at the decibel measure of some common sounds. Avoid listening to loud noises for long periods when possible.

Sound Source	Degree	Decibel Measure
Aircraft taking off	deafening	180
Thunder	deafening	120
Passing Truck	very loud	100
Lawn mower	very loud	100
Average traffic	loud	85
Washing Machine	loud	70
Average radio	loud	70
Conversation	moderate	60
Quiet stream	moderate	50

GO ON →

Source #2: Our Dark Night Sky, a Valuable Resource

When you step outside at night, can you see the stars shining in the sky? Or does the orange glow of city lights mask their sparkle? Today, some city skies are thousands of times brighter than 200 years ago. This increasing "light pollution" is a concern, because it affects our environment and wildlife.

Life Rhythms

Living things have adapted their habits to fit the daily cycles of light and darkness. For instance, certain animals, like bats, hunt for insects at night when fewer predators will see them. Unfortunately, light pollution can alter these cycles and cause far-reaching effects.

The Quest for Dinner

First, scientists say light pollution can change the timing of an animal's search for food. Some creatures wait until dusk to leave their homes and begin eating. When unexpected lights click on at sunset, the puzzled animals remain hidden and have less time to feed.

Light pollution influences where hungry animals hunt for meals, too. Because animals avoid lights to stay safe, they will pass by convenient meals in bright areas, wandering further to find food. The extra effort burns energy, requiring them to need more food.

Getting Together

Sometimes, light pollution disrupts the mating of animals. The firefly is one likely victim. Around the world, the numbers of this insect have dropped. Fireflies use flashing light patterns to attract mates in the dark. When the night sky is too bright, the blinking signals are difficult to notice, making it more challenging for fireflies to find each other.

Traveling Troubles

Often, light pollution causes problems for animals roaming at night. For instance, deer that encounter traffic cannot see well. Like many nocturnal animals, their eyes magnify light, and bright shining headlights blind them for a moment. Consequently, the deer may accidentally leap in front of a vehicle.

Other animals, like the puma, view the lighted highway like a fence. To survive, pumas require large territories for hunting. However, one scientist noted that when pumas neared lighted highways, they refused to cross. This most likely happened because the brightness hampered the puma's vision. Sadly, brightly lit areas are breaking apart the ranges where numerous animals travel, fragmenting their homes.

GO ON →

Light pollution creates dangerous confusion for traveling, newborn sea turtles, too. When they hatch, the turtles instantly seek the brightest light. In the past, moonlight reflecting on the ocean safely drew them into the water. Today, the gleam from beach homes bewilders the newborn turtles, and they aimlessly wander inland.

Migrating birds flying at night depend on both moonlight and the stars to navigate. However, a city's artificial glow sometimes blocks these guiding lights. Furthermore, shimmering buildings attract birds like magnets. Scientists do not understand why, but birds will circle the glittering building until exhausted. Airport towers and lighthouses present similar hazards.

How Can People Help?
Some big cities have started "Light Out" programs to help birds; building owners voluntarily shut off unnecessary lights during migration seasons. In addition, cities near beaches have passed laws guiding the usage and types of outside lights that people install.

You can reduce the problem by making wise choices in your own home and yard. First, avoid landscape lighting if it is simply decorative. Next, be sure to shut off unneeded lights, or use a timing system. Finally, position lights so their beams shine downward, not into the sky.

Currently 19% of the electricity used in the world is for lights at night. By working together, we may be able to lessen this number and save our dark night sky.

GO ON →

Source #3: Understanding Dams

The following information is part of a presentation on the benefits and drawbacks of dams.

What is considered a dam?

- A dam is a man-made structure that stops the flow of water.

- Once a dam is created, an artificial lake forms behind it.

- In the United States, the National Inventory of Dams (NID) lists 66,000 river dams.

Dams serve multiple purposes

- Dams produce hydroelectricity, a clean, renewable form of energy.

- Dams supply water for crops and household needs

- Dams allow people to prevent flooding. Dams can control the release of river water.

- Mining operations use dams to catch any pollution they create, so the pollution does not spread into rivers.

- Dams create large lakes for fish.

- Dams provide a new habitat for wildlife.

- Nearly 40% of all dams in our nation are used for recreation

GO ON →

Dams have drawbacks . . .

- Dams block rivers and limit debris such as twigs, leaves, and mud. Living things depend on debris for food and shelter.

- Dams stop river water from flowing downstream, reducing the depth of the stream. Shallow streams supply less water to the earth, and the groundwater level drops, affecting plants that depend on it.

- A dam's artificial lake floods plants and vegetation once used by wildlife.

- Dams block migrating fish from traveling upstream to lay eggs, and they prevent newly hatched fish from traveling downstream to oceans.

Photo courtesy of USDA Natural Resources Conservation Service

. . . but people are searching for solutions

People are working to solve problems created by dams. Fish "ladders" allow fish to travel around dams. Dams that are no longer useful are removed.

Photo by Gary Wilson, USDA Natural Resources Conservation Service

GO ON →

1 Pollution can change animal behaviors and their environments.

Complete the chart to show which sentence from Source #1, and which sentence from Source #2 **best** support this idea.

Best supports the idea	Source #1
☐	"In time, few seedlings were found near wells."
☐	"Today, scientists continue to investigate the impacts of noise pollution."
☐	"In some cases, low-flying planes frighten herds of animals, causing stampedes."
	Source #2
☐	"To survive, pumas require large territories for hunting."
☐	"When they hatch, the turtles instantly seek the brightest light."
☐	"Around the world, the numbers of this insect have dropped."

GO ON →

Name: _____ Date: _____

2 Explain how making changes in our environment can reduce the negative impact on plants and animals living around us. Give **two** examples, one from Source #1, one from Source #2. For each example, include the source title or number.

_____

_____

_____

_____

_____

3 In Source #3, the author provides examples of the positive and negative aspects of dams and their effect on the environment. Explain how this provides a different point of view from the other **two** sources. Use details from the text to support your answer.

_____

_____

_____

_____

_____

GO ON →

Directions for Part 2

You will now review your notes and sources, and plan, draft, revise, and edit your opinion article. You may use your notes and refer to the sources as often as you need.

Now read your assignment and the information about how your writing will be scored; then begin your work.

Your Assignment:

Your town is considering building a new, faster highway system that will save the townspeople time and money. The highway will be built over an existing swamp and includes plans for a new dam. As editor of your school newspaper, you are going to write a multi-paragraph article giving your opinion about this proposal. In your article, you will take a side as to whether you think the idea is a good one or whether it should be reconsidered. The audience for your article will be the students at your school, parents, and your community. In your article, clearly state your opinion and support your opinion with reasons that are thoroughly developed using information from what you have read. Choose the most important information from all three sources to support your ideas. Then, write an opinion article that is several paragraphs long. Clearly organize your article and support your ideas with details from the sources. Use your own words except when quoting directly from the sources. Be sure to give the source title when using details from the sources.

REMEMBER: A well-written opinion article

- has a clear opinion
- is well-organized and stays on the topic
- has an introduction and conclusion
- uses transitions
- uses details or facts from more than one source to support your opinion
- gives details or facts from the sources in your own words
- gives the title or number of the source for the details or facts you included
- develops ideas clearly
- uses clear language
- follows rules of writing (spelling, punctuation, and grammar usage)

Now begin work on your opinion article. Manage your time carefully so that you can plan, write, revise, and edit the final draft of your article. Write your response on a separate sheet of paper.

Answer Key

Name: _____

Question	Correct Answer	Content Focus	CCSS	Complexity
1	C, E	Synonyms	L.5.5c	DOK 2
2	D	Personification	L.5.5a	DOK 2
3	C, F	Text Structure: Problem and Solution	RI.5.5	DOK 2
4	C	Context Clues: Paragraph Clues	L.5.4a	DOK 2
5	B	Synonyms and Antonyms	L.5.5c	DOK 2
6	A	Cause and Effect	RI.5.3	DOK 2
7	see below	Text Features: Illustrations	RI.4.7	DOK 3
8A	B	Point of View	RL.5.6	DOK 3
8B	D	Point of View/ Text Evidence	RL.5.6/ RL.5.1	DOK 3
9	See below	Context Clues: Paragraph Clues	L.5.4a	DOK 2
10	D, E	Literary Element: Descriptive Details	RL.5.4	DOK 2
11A	B	Literary Element: Flashback	RL.5.5	DOK 3
11B	A	Literary Element: Flashback/ Text Evidence	RL.5.5/ RL.5.1	DOK 3
12	D	Point of View	RL.5.6	DOK 2
13A	C	Theme	RL.5.2	DOK 3
13B	B	Theme/Text Evidence	RL.5.2/ RL.5.1	DOK 3
14	see below	Theme	RL.5.2	DOK 3
15	see below	Homophones	L.5.4	DOK 2
16	B	Cause and Effect	RI.5.3	DOK 2
17	see below	Text Structure: Problem and Solution	RI.5.5	DOK 3
18	D	Personification	L.5.5a	DOK 2
19	C	Point of View	RL.5.6	DOK 2
20	see below	Literary Element: Flashback	RL.5.5	DOK 2
21	see below	Compare Across Texts	W.5.9	DOK 4

Answer Key

Name: _____

Question	Correct Answer	Content Focus	CCSS	Complexity
22	D	Prepositional Phrases as Adjectives and Adverbs	L.5.1a	DOK 1
23	D	Adverbs that Compare	L.5.1	DOK 1
24	A	Negatives	L.5.1	DOK 1
25	A	Sentence Combining	L.5.5	DOK 1
26	B	Sentence Combining	L.5.1	DOK 1
27	B	Prepositional Phrases as Adjectives and Adverbs	L.5.1a	DOK 1
28	C	Negatives	L.5.1	DOK 1
29	B	Adverbs	L.5.1	DOK 1
30	C	Adverbs that Compare	L.5.1	DOK 1
31	A	Adverbs	L.5.1	DOK 1

Comprehension: Selected Response 3, 6, 8A, 8B, 10, 11A, 11B, 12, 13A, 13B, 16, 19	/18		%
Comprehension: Constructed Response 7, 14, 17, 20, 21	/12		%
Vocabulary 1, 2, 4, 5, 9, 15, 18	/14		%
English Language Conventions 22–31	/10		%
Total Unit Assessment Score	/54		%

7 **2-point response:** The author realizes not everyone is familiar with this medium and wants it to seem more real and to help people see how detailed the art can be. This makes it more likely that readers will come to the show and get to appreciate pen and ink drawing and the work of the club.

9 Students should match the following:
• eternity: a long time
• massive: larger than usual

14 **2-point response:** The message of this story is that nothing is lost by being kind, but something is gained. Jesse does not want to invite Michael because he does not "know him very well at all." Jesse has a change of heart when he realizes that he himself once felt alone like Michael. After the party, Jesse is happy about his decision and has found a new friend.

15 Students should match the following:
• ordinary; common: plane
• to see how heavy something is: way

17 **2-point response:** Most pilots were men, and people thought women should not do long flights or fly as a career. Amelia did not listen to these people. She joined a female pilot organization and started flying long distances. She also had to sell her plane to give her mother money, so flying became a hobby for a while.

20 **2-point response:** The reader learns that Jason was nervous during his first game. Also, the reader learns that practicing at home was not all Jason needed in order to be a good player. He had to work all the time to improve his playing. This helps show how important and special the game of basketball is to him.

21 **4-point response:** Jason's family did not think he would be able to play basketball with a prosthetic leg. Jason plays anyway and shows everyone that he can do anything others can do. Amelia pilots a plane at a time when planes have not been around for long and many people believe women should not fly. She shows that women can do everything men can do by setting records and taking daring flights.

Both can be role models for others who want to follow in their footsteps. Both focus on a goal and work toward it. Both seem to love what they do. Both texts show that people's abilities can surprise people who do not believe in them. Both characters show how important it is to recognize the abilities of others.

Answer Key

Name: _____

Opinion Performance Task				
Question	**Answer**	**CCSS**	**Complexity**	**Score**
1	see below	RI.5.1, RI.5.2, RI.5.3, RI.5.7, RI.5.8, RI.5.9 W.5.1a-d, W.5.2, W.5.4, W.5.7 L.5.1, L.5.2	DOK 2	/1
2	see below		DOK 3	/2
3	see below		DOK 3	/2
Opinion Article	see below		DOK 4	/4 [P/O] /4 [E/E] /2 [C]
Total Score				/15

1 Students should select the following:
- Source #1: "An Invisible Pollution": "In time, few seedlings were found near wells."
- Source #2: "Our Dark Night Sky, a Valuable Resource": "To survive, pumas require large territories for hunting."

2 **2-point response:** People can help reduce the negative impact we have our plants and animals by making changes. In Source #1: "An Invisible Pollution," the author points out that turning down the volume on machines and shutting of things we aren't using can help. In Source #2: "Our Dark Night Sky," the author notes that many people are turning off lights they are not using to avoid confusing birds and other flying animals, especially when they are migrating.

3 **2-point response:** In Source #1: "An Invisible Pollution" and Source #2: "Our Dark Night Sky," the authors discuss how man-made changes have created a negative impact on the environment. However, in Source #3: "Understanding Dams," while the author explains the benefits of dams to people, and ways to retain this resource while limiting its effect on the environment.

Answer Key

Name: _____

10-point anchor paper: Currently, our county is debating whether or not to build a new highway outside of town. People are concerned about how this will affect the wildlife in the area, and for good reason. The new highway could change the behaviors of many animals living nearby. However, we have learned so much about how light and noise affect wildlife, surely we can find solutions to the problems this project presents. The best time to build this highway is now, when the community is thinking about the impact on the environment. That way, we can find ways to make the highway have less of an impact on local wildlife.

Since we have learned a great deal about how light from highways affects the environment, perhaps we can find a solution for this, such as motion-activated streetlights or an unlighted overpass for animals. That way, animals like the puma will not see the highway as a boundary that limits where it can travel for food. Motion-activated lights would also save energy and be less likely to confuse migrating birds.

The noise of construction and of vehicles on the new highway is also a significant issue, but since we know that, perhaps we can find ways to limit the effect of this noise on the environment. For example, plants and dirt banks could soak up most of the noise before it travels far from the road.

Finally, the construction of a new dam will have a large impact on the environment. Because much of the water from the wetland will be contained in the dammed area, volunteers will be needed to move some plants and animals to the new wetland area. This may preserve species that otherwise might not survive. Finally, if we use our dam as a clean energy source, we can reduce noise and light created by other power sources.

Some may say that these steps do not solve the whole problem. However, I believe our goal should be to try to live in harmony with the environment. Given the lifestyle people are used to and will insist on, this will have to happen in a series of small steps, like what I've described above. Quite simply, there is no way to erase the mark we have made on the environment, so we need to act as its caretakers now. That means thinking carefully about how our actions will impact it and taking steps to preserve it, even as progress pushes us forward.